Developing Positive Self-Images and Discipline in Black Children

by Jawanza Kunjufu

AFRICAN AMERICAN IMAGES
Chicago, Illinois

Cover design by Eugene Winslow

Photo credits: Kawana Emerson Sherman

Second edition, thirteenth printing

Copyright © 2000 by Jawanza Kunjufu
(*Kiswahili for dependable & cheerful*)

DEDICATION

This book is dedicated to Vergeous Gillam who encouraged me to put my major workshop, also in cassette, into book format. It is also dedicated to all African-American children who I believe have a message to tell if only we will listen.

SPECIAL THANKS

Special thanks is given to Eugene Winslow, and Schavi Diarra for their editorial assistance. A special thanks is given to Na'im Akbar for the introduction and editorial advice. Deep respect and appreciation are given to Sanyika Anwisye and Kawana Emerson Sherman for their scholarship lended to the book. Sincere gratitude is given to Vera Brent and my mother, Mary Brown, for their technical contributions.

COMMITMENT

And on this day, we commit our children to African American excellence. Guide us, to give our children wisdom and responsibility, so they as African children before them, will ride on a camel to the African paradise, "Ahera". And if we fail, may our children denounce us, and our names be forgotten, for as long as the sun shines and the water flows.

Table of Contents

Introduction

My objective in writing *Developing Positive Self-Images and Discipline in Black Children* is to look at the complete child and all the factors that potentially affect their future. The six chapters— "The Politics of Educating Black Children," "Developing Positive Self-Images and Self-Esteem in Black Children," "A Relevant Curriculum," "Self-Discipline," "Parenting: Children Are the Reward of Life," and "From Theory to Practice: Strategies for Success,"— are broad and extensive enough to warrant their own individual book.

I believe in the holistic approach to solve most problems, and particularly positive images and self-discipline in Black children. My major recommendations to achieve the title of this book are:
  (1) To recognize that a problem exists in the development of African-American children, and to analyze why and by whom the problem is perpetuated.
  (2) African-American children need to be given a frame of reference that is consistent with their culture. Our children should analyze images, literature, history, etc., from an African frame of reference.
  (3) Our children should be encouraged to maintain their curiosity and enthusiasm to learn. I feel this can be achieved with a curriculum that mandates thinking skills.
  (4) Self-discipline results from consistent adult role models that are complementary and assertive.
  (5) The first and primary teachers of children are parents who should develop a home program which enhances the development of the child's talents and increases the parent's possibility of developing responsible adults.
  (6) We must advocate and possess high expectations for the best services available to our children, create supplemental programs, and build independent institutions which further enhance the possibilities of developing positive self-images and discipline in Black children.
The following six chapters provide a review of the literature available on each concept, and support the respective premises listed above. I mentioned previously that each chapter warrants its own book; the same applies to the three audiences I've attempted to address—teachers, parents, and educational researchers in that order.

The book also reflects my workshop audience. It is also an appeal to the reader to view himself in the same manner. Many teachers are also parents, but could improve their teacher-parent relationships. Teachers also are professionals, and should continue to keep abreast of the research in their field. Parents are the first teachers of children, and their home becomes the first classroom, yet many parents do not plan exercises for their children, nor keep abreast of the classwork brought home daily. Parents often read about their career development, but little on child development research. Educational scholars frequently have drifted so far away from the classroom they used to teach in and the home where they used to raise children that they have often been unable to relate theoretical paradigms to teachers and parents faced with developing children in the twenty-first century.

The book also encompasses theories from a broad perspective. I do not believe the problem is simply black and white; it may be easier to describe but it would not be accurate. I do believe that the integration of schools has reduced the expectations placed on Black students, but I do not believe that all White teachers are bad and all Black teachers are good. The readings of Malcolm X have taught me "by any means necessary." Therefore if White scholars such as John Goodlad, William Glasser, Rudolf Flesch, and Neil Postman can help me develop positive self-images and discipline in Black children, then I want to incorporate their knowledge with Asa Hilliard, Amos Wilson, Janice Hale, Na'im Akbar and other Black scholars.

Jawanza Kunjufu

Foreword

The problem of educating Black children in the American context is as old as the presence of Blacks in this setting. The question is also as complex as the experience of the African-American. Notables such as Dr. W.E.B. DuBois, Bishop Henry M. Turner, Dr. Carter G. Woodson, Marcus Garvey, Elijah Muhammad and Dr. Martin Luther King, Jr. have all addressed the issue of education as being one of fundamental importance in the progress of African-Americans. The example of Booker T. Washington, Mary McCleod Bethune, Dr. Benjamin Mays and many others are legendary in their commitment to developing institutions for the express purpose of educating Black youth. Frankly, Black history in America is completely imseparable from the attempt to handle the challenge of Black education in this setting of historical oppression and thwarted opportunity.

Many contemporary Black scholars have continued to address this same question of educating the African-American child. The inescapable reality is, and always has been, that the liberation of African-Americans is dependent upon an *effective* education. We emphasize "effective" because so much of our education has been virtually useless in accomplishing the objective of liberation. The process of "miseducation" as described by Dr. Carter G. Woodson in 1931 has continued to impede our progress as an educated people. Dr. Woodson's conclusion that the majority of educated Blacks were all but "worthless in the uplift of their people," remains an issue of deadly accuracy. His analysis was that the seat of the trouble was in what African-Americans were being taught.

The ancient function of education was to do no less than to develop positive self-images and discipline for the adherents of the educational system. The assumption that existed in those times of greater illumination than these was that the human being was already equipped with the tools of enlightenment. The word education did not assume that critical knowledge had to be imposed from without, but as the word itself implies, it was to be educed from within. The method for educing knowledge was done through the cultivation of an inner discipline which brought these resources to the fore. In Ancient Kemit (called Egypt) the original teachers cultivated self-esteem or a positive self-knowledge by fostering an awareness of ones historical (and/or mythological) origins which gave insight into the resources that each individual contained by virtue of his Divine and genetic legacy. The secret for such enlightenment was the Ancient Edict of "Man know thyself," inscribed by these ancient scholars on the portals of their Temples (which were simultaneously universities). The positive self-image emerged from the cultivation of self-knowledge. The application of the knowledge which was obtained was manifested through self-discipline. So the things most critical in an educational system is to know oneself, and to know how to manage that self. This persisting deficiency in the education of African-Americans has created the great difficulties of re-ascendency which we have experienced as a people. Dr. Woodson's identification of our problem as existing in what we were taught seems to still be a quite relevant assessment of our educational difficulties.

This problem described so accurately by Dr. Woodson over fifty years ago is even more of a problem as we enter the twenty-first century and find African-American youth being not only "miseducated" but actually "de-educated." De-educated means that they are being systematically excluded from the educational system and/or being systematically destroyed within that system. This is an issue of great complexity and magnitude, and it takes a thinker of considerable talent to tackle the numerous dimensions of this problem. Jawanza Kunjufu is such a thinker and this book addresses the issue of Black education in a very readable and pragmatic way.

Jawanza Kunjufu organizes his approach to Black education around the issue of the importance of positive self-images and discipline as a prerequisite for the effective education of African-American children. He takes a fresh approach to the age-old problem of self-esteem and its impact on education. This fresh approach is one which begins to analyze the source of self-esteem problems for African-American children and begins to propose some concrete resolutions for those problems.

One of the intriguing things about Jawanza Kunjufu's approach is that he lays a foundation for the unique problems which African-Americans face in the educational system. He discusses the political meaning of Black education, such as the media and the school's curriculum. Then his solutions are ones which have relevance to the education of all children. What he proposes as a relevant curriculum and appropriate teaching techniques are not approaches that have any particular unique applicability to African-Americans. The major hindrances to effective Black education, he apparently views as consistent with the problems of American education in general. He attributes at least part of the Black educational problem to the "banking concept" in education, the "certainty principle," rote learning, and several other major criticisms which non-Black writers have advanced about contemporary education in general. The interesting thing about this approach is that it sees the Black educational problem as a specific problem that is apparently aggravated by occurring in the context of an educational system that is already grossly inadequate even for the people it has been constructed to serve.

Despite this general analysis and suggestions geared towards correcting these general educational problems, he doesn't neglect the specific needs of the African-American child within this context. He addresses the unique cultural and learning styles of African-American children and the need for the curriculum to take those styles into account.

In addition to the problem of self-esteem, Jawanza Kunjufu addresses the problem of discipline confronting children in general, and specifically discipline as it relates to the African-American child. Again, he draws upon the contemporary issues of declining discipline within the educational and home environments while demonstrating the unique meaning of this problem for African-Americans. He maintains an analytical perspective which views the African-American child as emanating from a cultural and value base that is fundamentally different from the European-American cultural base. This perspective gives Kunjufu's discussion a solvency which far exceeds similar discussions by educator's who persist in seeing African-Americans as "no different" from Europeans. At the same time, the argument put forth is neither pat nor myopic. He identifies the interactive impact of being Black and American.

Again, in addressing solutions to the discipline problem, he draws upon the best of the African ethos, e.g., the importance of a spiritual orientation as the foundation for discipline. He also utilizes the pragmatic ethos of the Western world by even suggesting uses for the behavioral technology of Skinner. Such freedom from ideological constraint gives Kunjufu's proposed solutions a viability and applicability which far-exceeds more rigid approaches.

The range of problems which are discussed in this volume is vast. From self-esteem to child management by African-American single mothers, the issues are as contemporary as tomorrow. The problems are not only contemporary but are begging for solutions as they threaten to disintegrate the future survival of African-Americans. Though Jawanza Kunjufu's ideas are far from complete in resolving these problems, they can certainly be helpful. The book is a manual describing some techniques which teachers, parents and others who plan the work with children might apply in addressing some specific adjustment difficulties of African-American children. The author seems to be cognizant of the fact that these particular difficulties exist in a social matrix rooted in oppression, thwarted opportunity violated human freedom and European ethnocentrism. He also recognizes that these problems of African-American youth are part of an educational system that is too materialistic, too individualistic, and too mechanistic. Though this context is clear, he succeeds in going beyond the limits of what-cannot-be-done and shows us some real things that can be done until the oppressive context is vanquished. This fact alone makes this document a must reading for those who ask: "But, what can we do about it . . . ?"

Na'im Akbar
Professor
Florida State University

Chapter 1
The Politics
of Educating Black Children

The major objective of writing *Developing Positive Self-Images and Discipline in Black Children* is because these character traits are not presently being developed. I believe the first step at solving any problem is to recognize its existence, and determine its perpetuators and their motive. The difficulties African-American children face are best described in a Chicago newspaper article about the low-income area housing project, Cabrini Green:

> After school the children started drifting into the Cabrini-Green branch library. One of the first was Ronnell Fant, 9, a boy who skips instead of walks. Ronnell, nose running, darted around like a minnow. He played and talked to friends he said he wants to be a doctor.

> Giggly, outspoken Gwendolyn Terry, 9, is a regular, too. She wants to be a singer. Marletta, 11, another regular, brought her little sister. Marletta never removed her stained, threadbare coat. Her sister's dress was faded and dirty. Her hair needed combing. In contrast to Gwendolyn's cheery confidence, these girls were wary and silent. Marletta wants to be a beautician.

> Tina Hayes, 12, already has a job. With her sisters and cousins, she delivers newspapers to 200 Gold Coast apartments each day before school. She also wants to be a singer.

> Doctor, singer, beautician. What are the chances that their ambitions will become reality? These Cabrini-Green children are midway between innocence and realism, clinging to dreams but savvy enough to see that the projects are more dangerous than the neighborhoods they read about in the library storybooks. Each has heard stories about gang violence and rape. A few, the neglected ones, are rearing themselves and each other. A few others use the elevator at the end of the hall as a toy, endangering themselves and everyone else. But it is safe to say that everyone beyond the age of 8 or 9 is beginning to know the effects of cramming too many people with too little money and too few dreams into one housing project.

Their lives begin sweetly, and most very young children show no indication of the cheated feeling that will come later. Motasha McGill, 3, sees only loving parents and a happy day in nursery school. "I love my mommy. I wouldn't trade her for anything," she said with an engaging smile.[1]

These children talk about the future the same way other children do. But most other children have more money in their families, get more encouragement in school, and are part of a community that does not feel that they are born to fail.

The Record of Miseducation

Forty-two percent of all Black children seventeen years old can't read beyond a sixth-grade reading level.[2] The Black high-school student drop out rate is 49.6 percent.[3] Black children are 17 percent of the school population, but make up 41 percent of the EMR (Educable Mentally Retarded) students, and if a Black child is labeled EMR or BD (Behavioral Disorder) 85 percent of the time it will be a Black boy.[4]

The frightening reality is that an increasing number of Black youth and adults will never work. Sidney Wilhelm in *Who Needs the Negro*[5] raises the historical question, Why were Africans brought to this country? He answers by saying to work. He then asks the contemporary and futuristic question, Does that reason exist today and tomorrow? The answer is a resounding *no*. Between now and the start of the twenty-first century, the number of youth is expected to decline about 30 percent, while the total for Black and Hispanic will hold steady. At the same time, the type of low-skill, entry-level industrial jobs traditionally filled by young men will shrink. Despite the continued growth of teenage pregnancies, labor participation rates of young Black women are expected to increase from about 55 percent today to more than 70 percent. This increase will parallel young white women's rates. Most young Black men are simply not counted in the labor statistics, and they've been falling out since the mid-1950s. If the total of non-participants is added to the officially unemployed, it means fewer than half of Black men under twenty-four have a job today, and fewer than a third will hold a job at the turn of the century. Entry-level and low-skill industrial jobs, traditionally filled by young men, will decline while clerical positions operated with 80 percent females is increasing.[6]

The last time the Black community had full employment was during slavery. It has been estimated that throughout the years of European and Arab invasions, 250 million Africans have died either defending themselves or committing suicide before submitting to slavery. I remember in the early seventies, providing a cultural assembly to children, dramatizing the strength of those 250 million to refute the historical picture that our ancestors were docile and submissive. Afterwards, a brother suggested I emphasize more the five million who survived and accepted slavery for the moment, in hopes that future generations would be free. While all Africans form our ancestry, our direct lineage stems from the 5 million. I accepted his analysis, but my concern is our desire to *survive* may be our *only* desire. Anderson Thompson, a noted professor at Northeastern University, once commented, "Cockroaches survive, men and women develop." You often hear Blacks say to each other "I'm just trying to make it, to hang in there." I just don't believe that our ancestors envisioned their future having such limited aspirations hundreds of years later. That's why history is so important, because if our children had been taught correctly, they would have a burning spirit for freedom, liberation, and self-actualization. Our children need to know what our ancestors experienced. They need to know slaves were beaten if found reading or learning how to write. History is not a subject that keeps children memorizing dates and events of the past, but is the study making contemporary decisions and future predictions based on historical data. Relevant historical questions include; What can we learn from our ancestors that we can use right now? Our ancestors valued an education; the brilliance demonstrated in Africa and the threat of death in slavery if found studying should inspire our youth. We have failed to fuel our children with a burning spirit to do more than survive and "make it." We have not developed positive historical images that give our children self-images and discipline.

Tanzanian President Julius Nyerere notes,

> The purpose of education is to transmit from one generation to the next the accumulated wisdom and knowledge of the society, and prepare children for their future participation in the maintenance and development of the society. With the advent of colonial rule this changed. A formal system of education was introduced, the function of which was not to prepare children for service to the community in which they lived, but rather to produce servants to the colonial administration.[7]

This is the politics in educating Black children. What do we see when we look at our children? It is believed that what we see and expect in our children will be the results. Do we see future employers? Do we see future mayors, presidents and engineers?

The Manipulation of Childhood

The period called childhood has gone through many changes in western culture. What is childhood? What makes it distinct from adulthood? How long should childhood last? What determines the end of childhood? Who determines it's over? Martin Hoyles in *Changing Childhood* comments,

> The invention of childhood as a separate state corresponds with the transition from feudalism to capitalism. The first modern children were middle class and male, and this fact is significant. Girls could learn their future work in the home and so did not have to go to school. Similarly, it is clear from the way working class children had to work in the mines, potteries and mills that there were no childhood for them. On the land too, as John Locke observed in 1697, the children of the poor had to work for some part of the day from the age of three. The crucial separation which modern children suffer is the separation from work. Before the industrial revolution most work was done in or around the home and the household was an economic unit. But by the nineteenth century the factory system had eliminated many of the production functions of the family. Work had become split from family life, threatening its disruption. This is why the early working class defended child labor, it preserved the traditional ties between children and their parents, particularly their fathers who taught them a skill. When a class of six year olds in a London school were asked to draw pictures of adults and children, they drew the following activities:

Adults	Children
Painting	Jumping up and down
Washing the floor	Playing with a car
Driving a car	Flying a kite
Cleaning windows	Kicking a football
Preparing dinner	Playing cowboys and indians
Washing dishes	Watching Bugs Bunny
Sewing	Going to school
Cutting the grass	Drawing

> Significantly, the children are all playing and the adults are working, but the work they are doing is domestic work as the children are cut off from seeing the work which their parents go out to do.[8]

Childhood, education, and the economy are intricately related. Schools are designed to produce labor power according to the demands of capital, by making differentiated school knowledge available to advantaged and disadvantaged groups. This in turn reproduces hierarchy, exclusion, and inequality between social classes and ethnic groups. Schools have accomplished this social reproduction, in part, by presenting certain knowledge to certain groups. Schools do not offer the same curriculum or provide the same equipment locally, statewide, or nationally. Mississippi, for example, primarily depends on cotton, and remains the only state with no compensatory education laws, allowing them to draw upon cheap labor.

The economy is not the only factor that has shaped the image of childhood; Neil Postman in the *Disappearance of Childhood* remarks:

> Every educated person knows about the invasions of the northern bar-barians, the collapse of the Roman empire, the shrouding of classical culture, the Europe's descent into what is called the Dark and then the Middle Ages. Our textbooks cover the transformation well enough except for four points that are often overlooked and that are particularly relevant to the story of childhood. The first is that literacy disappears. The second is that education disappears. The third is that shame disappears. And the fourth, as a conse-quence of the other three, is that childhood disappears. In an oral world there is not much of a concept of an adult and therefore, even less of a child. And that is why, in all the sources, one finds that in the Middle Ages childhood ended at age seven. Why seven? Because that is the age at which children have command over speech. They can say and understand what adults can say and understand. They are able to know all the secrets of the tongue, which are the only secrets they need to know. A new communication environment began to take form in the sixteenth century as a result of prin-ting and social literacy. The printing press created a new definition of adulthood, based on reading competence, and corresponding, a new concep-tion of childhood based on reading incompetence. Prior to the coming of that new environment, infancy ended at seven and adulthood began at once.[9]

Developing positive self-images and discipline will remain dif-ficult if we are not clear on the distinction between childhood and adulthood. Children who grow up too fast will lack the respect for elders and vital information to achieve this goal. In contrast, the new technological economy has lengthened the period called childhood. Many children are bored and view themselves as non-productive and inactive, with no political and economic strength. The national government confirms the lack of political clout of children by cutting Homestart, Headstart, Chapter I, and CETA, and by increasing prison sentences, the number of prisons, and law enforcement personnel. The complex combination of parents work-ing away from home, massive youth unemployment, and ineffec-tive schools, while at the same time childhood is being prolonged by the economy constrained by its shifting from print to electronic medias has created high levels of frustration among all parties. The present economy of post-industrialism — computer, typewriter, word processor, service sector — does not need the large labor pool demanded by its predecessor, the factory. The economy is now placing greater emphasis on quality for the few, rather than mediocrity for the masses. A different curriculum is needed to design a computer program versus placing widget 186 on top of a widget 185. The former economy requires more information, but fewer people. The dilemma is that the remaining children who now live in large cities see the American dream, but live the American nightmare.

In the article "Save the Children," Atkinson and Horde state,

> Every educational system functions to perpetuate the larger society by acculturating its young into that order, and the purpose of the American colonial education system is to maintain this societal structure. its claims of individual freedom, cultural pluralism and world democratization obscure its ideologies of elitism, cultural monism, and world Americanization; and Black children are the acculturated victims. Let's define terms:
>
> *Elitism:* Those who achieve or fail to achieve self-realization, the aggrandizement of status and material wealth are responsible for their own success or failure.
>
> *Cultural Monism:* Anglo-Saxon cultural production and values represent standards by which to measure all cultural production and values.
>
> *World Americanization:* This is elitism at the national level, the idea that the hegemony of the United States over other nations is a consequence of this country being the fittest.
>
> These structural realities contribute to the academic and cultural problems of Black students; miseducated to believe in individual freedom, and that one is thus repsonsible for one's own success or failure. Black students often question their own intelligence when they do not succeed in school.[10]

The above analysis has divided the Black intellectual community. Authors like Thomas Sowell and William Wilson are encouraged by the white elite to "blame the victim" and to demonstrate that the reason "some of us" have made it is due to hard work and effort. The ticklish issue is that Atkinson, Horde, myself, and a host of others are not discouraging hard work and effort, but we do question whether it was hard work and effort that made one percent of the population the ruling class in the United States. There are approximately 600,000 millionaires and 13 billionaires in the USA. Forty percent of corporate directors are members of the ruling class, and 60 percent of the top 300 corporations are controlled by ruling class families. The ruling class is organized into family groups, usually marry each other, and go to their own exclusive schools and social clubs while avoiding the public media. Fifty-five percent of the corporate board

"Black children must receive competency in mastering the tools of their cultures if they are to survive."

members and executives were educated at twelve prestigious universities. The rulers own 62 percent of all corporate stock, while the top 20 percent of the population owns 91 percent of all stock. The ruling class inherits its wealth from previous generations who accumulated it at the expense of the masses of American people.[11]

Does America want to educate all of its children? Does America want to employ all of its people? Is the lack of hard work and effort the explanation for thousands of workers waiting in lines responding to rumors of job openings? These are the political questions of education. Janice Hale answers,

> The American educational system has a dual purpose for educating Black children. The first is socializing them into accepting the value system, history and culture of Anglo-Americans. The second is education for economic productivity. Black children are treated like commodities to be imbued with skills which are bought and sold on the labor market for the profit of the capitalists.

The educator in the struggle for liberation also has dual purposes for educating the oppressed. The two purposes of education for the liberator are education for struggle and education for survival. Education for struggle, has a consciousness raising function for Black people. This facet of education tells us: Who we are, who the enemy is, what he is doing to us, when to fight, when to stop fighting, what to struggle for and what form the struggle must take. Education for struggle is long range because Black people must become prepared to make a contribution to a struggle that began centuries before we were born and which will extend for centuries after our death. Education for survival is the tooling function of education. Black children must receive competency in mastering the tools of this culture if they are to survive.[12]

I believe that to develop positive self-images and discipline in Black children requires this conscious-raising function.

In a conversation with a priest/principal of a Catholic Black male college preparatory high school, he informed me that his school was not interested in Black culture and that was why the curriculum reflected that position. Many thoughts raced through my mind; first, I suspected that the principal probably had no interest or commitment to "education for struggle"; second, I questioned how scientific his parent poll was to determine this view; third, I wondered if the rest of his curriculum was determined by the parents or *just* this area; and last, I confronted the sad reality that some Black parents do not see the need for Black culture, yet continually allow white culture to be taught. Many Black parents still view education as the three R's, and fail to see the significance of positive self-esteem, purpose, and cooperative values. Carter G. Woodson provides the missing link:

> In thus estimating the results obtained from the so-called education of the Negro the author does not go to the census figures to show the progress of the race. It may be of no importance to the race to be able to boast today of many times as many "educated" members as it had in 1865. If they are of the wrong kind the increase in numbers will be a disadvantage rather than an advantage. The only question which concerns us here is whether these "educated" persons are actually equipped to face the ordeal before them, or unconsciously contribute to their own undoing by perpetuating the regime of the oppressor. The problem of holding the Negro down, therefore is easily solved. When you control a man's thinking you do not have to worry about his actions. You do not have to tell him not to stand here or go yonder. He will find his "proper place," and will stay in it. You do not need to send him to the back door. He will go without being told. In fact, if there is no back door, he will cut one for his special benefit. His education makes it necessary. Negroes are trained exclusively in the psychology and economics of Wall Street and are, therefore, made to despise the opportunities to run ice wagons, push banana carts. Foreigners, who have not studied economics, but have studied Negroes, take up this business and grow rich. The greatest indictment of such education is that Negroes have thereby learned little as to making a living, the first essential in civilization.[13]

The level of self esteem, sense of purpose, and direction of parents is directly related to the child's performance. What do Black parents want for their children? An education? What kind of education? Segregated? Integrated? Separate but equal? Independent and alternative? Private? Who will make the decisions for Black children? Who will make the decisions for Black parents? Do the majority of Black parents want integration? This is the politics of educating Black children. Does the NAACP and the "talented tenth" represent the feelings of the masses? Is it worth discussing after *Brown* vs *Topeka Board of Education*, the closing of Black schools, Black principals becoming teachers, Black teachers being fired or transferred, a general decline in teacher competency and expectations, and parents unable to participate in their previously local community school versus the bused arrangements in suburbia?

The University of Chicago conducted a study of 70,000 schools trying to determine the major factor in student performance.[14] Much of the educational literature cites the importance of student's socioeconomic factors. Many reports describe performance related to the number of parents in the home, income and educational level. The University of Chicago notes that this is not the most important factor, but a distant third. The second most important factor and the rationale for integration was the school-per-pupil expenditure. Many educators and parents feel that the per-pupil expenditure is directly related to performance. Black parents, aware that white schools received a higher allocation, felt that by sending their child to a white school the same benefits would accrue to their children. For some parents money was the major rationale for busing. For others, being with white children and viewing the world in a manner similar to their future employment arena was felt to be advantageous. For others, it was simply the humanitarian thing to do, or because everyone else was doing it. The University reported school per-pupil expenditure is not the number one criteria. The most important factor in student performance is not parent demography or how much money the school has, but *teacher/parent expectations.*

Tuscaloosa, Alabama, 1920, one room school shack, forty Black students, roof leaking, only two books, but all forty students learned, because the teachers and parents expected it. My position, therefore, is that any decision concerning education should always take into consideration the expectation level of the teacher.

The general feeling nationwide is that expectations of both teachers and parents have declined. The reasons for the decline are numerous. Black parents, like all Americans, have been affected by the economy. Over the past sixty years, the economy has moved from agriculture to manufacturing to computerization. This has also changed the family structure from extended to nuclear to single. Alvin Toffler's *Third Wave* provides a more detailed analysis: 67 million people are single, and over 50 percent of all Black children live in a single parent home. The change in the economy has reduced the number of adults available, and also taken the breadwinner further from home. Please note, the author is very much aware that a third of the Black population is unemployed and living below the poverty line, and while they are nearer our children, their low self esteem presents additional problems. Parents, fewer in number and working further away, have steadily placed more burdens on schools to educate, console, and feed their children. A school strike in Chicago determined that, beyond the tragedy of students missing class, they were also being denied two of their best daily meals. The society has become so specialized, many parents are not confident talking with teachers about *their own* children, and complain about the teacher's condescending attitude. Teachers, feeling parents do not care, resent the increased responsibility. Some teachers also feel Black children can't learn regardless of their effort, consequently their self fulfilling prophecy becomes a reality. What I constantly hear nationwide are parents and teachers complaining *about* each other, but not *to* each other in a constructive manner that would bring about change. In the meantime, our children suffer from the poor, if any, communication between parents and teachers and from the policy decisions concerning integration. Developing positive self-images and discipline is greatly enhanced with high expectations and collaboration between teacher and parent.

Black children also suffer because school staff who have the power to label, classify, and define do not always have our children's best interest at heart. Lerone Bennett says:

> An educator in a system of oppression is either a revolutionary or an oppressor. The question of education for Black people in America is a question of life and death. It is a political question. A question of power. Struggle is a form of education — perhaps the highest form.[15]

This is a strong statement and leaves no room for interpretation. Unfortunately, our teachers who have high expectations for their children have those same sentiments for themselves. Increasingly, our better teachers are resigning because they are burned out from a frustrating situation, while on the other hand, teachers with lower expectations for the children and themselves often teach thirty years of mediocrity. Administrators should become sensitive to this dynamic and create dialog with these high-expectative teachers to develop greater levels of endurance. Janice Hale reinforces the need for Black child advocates:

> The Black community of educational and psychological scholars must consider seriously the importance of the struggle for the control of the research that is done with our children. We must recognize the role of educational research in our struggle for definition. The struggle for research is indeed the struggle for definition. The power to define is the power to destroy. If one has the power to define your child as being mentally retarded, then one has the power to sentence him to special classes for the rest of his academic career.[16]

This is the politics of educating Black children, and its effect on positive images and self-discipline.

Manipulation Tactics

The major catalyst for *Countering the Conspiracy to Destroy Black Boys* was in visiting classrooms, I witnessed a disproportionate number of boys placed by teachers in EMR classes (Educable Mentally Retarded). When I asked teachers if this was coincidental, the most frequent response was, "If you knew how bad these boys acted you would do the same or suspend them yourself." These are the same teachers who will complain about street crime and no available men for themselves or their daughters, but see no conflict in sentencing primary and intermediate boys to classes which have a poor track record in developing academic achievement.

Standardized ability testing has become big business in the United States, estimated at $500 million annually. It is estimated that more than fifty million American children take at least three standardized tests a year. Two of the most thoroughly researched concepts in psychology are those of intelligence and achievement testing. Yet, these phenomena are two of the most ill-used and grossly abused procedures employed in the assessment of intelligence and school achievement in Black children. Conventional ability tests often improperly label and classify Black children. Thus, if a Black child scores low on a test that is biased, and if he is placed (or misplaced) in an educational tract program because he scored low, then that child is trapped in a vicious circle known as the "Rosenthal Effect" or the self-fulfilling prophecy. It may not be the child's ability that keeps him in a lower tract, but adult's lowered expectations derived from test scores. There is an erroneous equation made between IQ and intelligence; this error leads the general population to the false conclusion that Blacks are inferior to whites in ability. Moreover, it is ridiculous to think of inheriting an IQ, rather than exposure to environmental factors patterned to the test.

Psychologists have known for many years that ability tests are biased in favor of white, native-born American children, the population on whom the tests were standardized. These practices violate the three basic assumptions on which psychometric instruments are based i.e., validity, reliability and standardization. In addition, the legal and constitutional rights of the Black child are being seriously violated. The Association of Black Psychologists called for a moratorium on the administration of IQ tests to Black children. The association charged that tests:

1) Label Black children as uneducable.
2) Place Black children in special classes.
3) Potentiate inferior education.
4) Assign Black children to lower educational tracts than whites.
5) Deny Black children higher education opportunities.
6) Destroy positive growth and development of Black children.

Robert Williams developed an intelligence test that is biased in favor of Black people. The name of the instrument is the BITCH test, which is translated Black Intelligence Test Counterbalanced for Honkies.

Is it more indicative of intelligence to know Malcolm X's last name or the author of Hamlet? I ask you now when is Washington's birthday? Perhaps 99 percent of you thought February 22. The answer presupposes a white form. I actually meant Booker T. Washington's birthday, not George Washington's. What is the color of bananas? Many of you would say yellow. But by the time the banana has made it to my community, to the ghetto, it is brown with yellow spots. So I always thought bananas were brown. Again, I was penalized by the culture in which I live. What is the correct thing to do if another child hits you without meaning to do it? The response is determined by the neighborhood lived in. In my community, to walk away would mean suicide. For survival purposes, children in Black communities are taught to hit back; however that response receives zero credit on current intelligence tests such as the Stanford-Binet.

The Black child does quite well in coping with his home and neighborhood environment, but does poorly in the school system. He clearly shows every indication of brightness at home. It is incumbent upon educators to develop appropriate learning experiences in the classroom which relate to the Black child's background experiences and not the other way around.[17]

The problems educating Black children have reached, in my opinion, epidemic proportions, but I don't feel the urgency from all parties involved. I put a great deal of emphasis on the "Black middle class or the talented tenth" to provide the masses of our people with direction. Carter G. Woodson has already explained why our leadership so often fails, but I don't think DuBois had this current behavior in mind when he created the phrase. I have tried to wrestle with why the urgency is not there. One reason may be that a large portion of the Black middle class sends their children to private schools which cannot be compared with public school for numerous reasons, including the principal's ability to hire and fire, determine the student population and generally receive greater parental support. If Black leadership send their children to private schools, that means the masses of parents must articulate and advocate our children's positions without them. Black leaders are directly involved where their children attend, and may become indirectly involved in workshops in public schools and by advocating through professional organizations. The least Black leaders can do is advocate in public school, with the ultimate desire being the enrollment of their children in public school, and to maximize involvement.

*   *   *   *   *

This chapter has been a brief look at the political areas affecting African-American children, which included a statistical analysis, the relationship between the economy and schools, the changing patterns of childhood, elitism, the purpose of education, expectations, and the implications of achievement test and future placement. My objective is to develop positive self-images and discipline in Black children, which necessitates identifying all impediment factors and making them known to all concerned with achieving this objective. Teachers, parents, and researchers need to know the changing capital intensive technology has less need for labor, and can afford a twenty-five to fifty percent drop out rate. The increased exposure to television has reduced the period of childhood, and robbed children of some of the innocence, enthusiasm, and respect for elders, all essential in developing positive self-images and discipline.

Major questions which should be raised are: Does America want to educate all of its children? Does it provide the same education for all or does elitism exist? It becomes important that we come to grips with these questions and, if answered honestly, hopefully will motivate a self determination and an African frame of reference.

This worldview will counteract the onslaught of "misplacement" of our children and demand high expectations for all those who interact with African-American children. The first step in developing self-images and discipline in Black children is to determine how much we value it. If we do, and current research shows major deficiencies, every effort should be made to rectify it. The next chapter on self-images and esteem is the first response.

Questions/Exercises/Projects

1) What is the relationship between the one percent ruling class and the Trilateral Commission?

2) Describe the potential significance African history can have on African-American children.

3) Within the context of Neil Postman's book, *The Disappearance of Childhood*, and his analysis of children growing up too fast, I have listed experiences which should be matched with the recommended age level.

The child's determination of:	Age
1) hair style	____
2) clothing	____
3) bed time	____
4) opposite sex phone calls	____
5) television program selection	____
6) peer group selection	____
7) room design	____
8) dating	____
9) smoking	____

Chapter 2

Developing Positive Self-Images and Self-Esteem in Black Children

The words *self-esteem* and *images* are often mistakenly used interchangeably. *Self-esteem* is to possess a favorable opinion of oneself, while *image* is defined as a likeness symbol, mental picture or the reliving of a sensation in the absence of the original stimulus. Self-esteem should be viewed more as an end result, and self-images more as a process or catalyst affecting self-esteem. The objectives of this chapter are to better understand self-esteem, its relationship to performance, and the sources, institutions, and images which affect it. The major concern is to develop positive self-images in Black children.

Paul Berg of the University of South Carolina describes the self-concept as "the individual's understanding of the expectations of society and his peers, and the kinds of behavior which the individual selects as a style of life. People discover who they are and what they are from the ways in which they have been treated by those who surround them in the process of growing up."[1] Dr. Berg is emphasizing that each person tries to be the kind of person that he thinks his environment expects him to be. If his parents or his teacher show him that they think he is bright, he tries to meet this expectation, and he accordingly tends to achieve academically. Conversely, if the adults indicate by their remarks and their attitudes that they expect him to do poorly, he performs at a level in keeping with the adults' estimates of his ability almost regardless of his true ability. The development of self-esteem emerges from the first contact the child has with his family. These experiences in infancy lead gradually to an awareness of self, as maturational forces and environmental experiences shape self-concept and esteem.

15

Indications of Low Self-Esteem

Let's review the literature to better understand the relationship between environment and self-esteem. There is an overwhelming influence of the white dominate society on the self-concept of Black children. Research done as early as 1939 by Clark and Clark documented the negative and confused racial attitudes frequently expressed by Black children. The Black children who participated in the Clarks' studies usually expressed a preference for white dolls and they rejected the black dolls. The Clarks note that, "It is clear that the Negro child by age five is aware of the fact that to be colored in contemporary American society is a mark of inferior status."[2] Research conducted by Goodman in 1952 and Moreland in 1962 confirm the Clark findings. Research found Black children under five frequently manifest uneasiness because of their awareness of skin differences. Moreland, rather than using dolls, showed kindergarten children pictures of Black and white children and asked them which children they preferred as playmates. The study showed a preference for whites as expressed by the majority of subjects.[3] This research indicates that preference for whites by children of both races developed early, even before racial differences could be communicated. Such results can be interpreted to mean that learning to prefer whites comes through indirect rather than direct verbal instruction.

Children are extremely sensitive to the messages that are given by the people around them. They start by learning and sensing how people feel by the silent messages that they receive. Children can feel rejection and negative racial attitudes that affect their self concepts. A child's self-concept is learned. He senses, feels, and assigns meaning to external stimuli in his life. Alvin Poussiant states,

> Black children, like all children, come into the world victims of factors over which they have no control. In the looking glass of white society, the supposedly undesirable physical image of "Tar Baby" — black skin, wooly hair and thick lips — is contrasted unfavorably with the valued model of "Snow White," — white skin, straight hair and aquiline feature.[4]

More recent research by psychologists Susan Ward and John Braun has found that Black youngsters develop a greater self-esteem than in previous findings, and prefer people of their own color to whites.[5] These recent findings, while encouraging and probably a tribute to efforts engaged in the late 60's and early 70's, do not negate Black's over-disproportionate consumption of haircare and cosmetic products. The quest for self-esteem has been historically unstable and

often volatile. Hence, Black self-esteem is reflective of a situation
DuBois described well over eighty years ago:

> This double-consciousness, this sense of always looking at one's self through
> the eye of others, of measuring one's soul by the tape of a world that looks on
> in amused contempt and pity. One ever feels his twoness, — an American, a
> Negro; two souls, two thoughts, two unreconciled strivings, two warring
> ideals in one dark body, whose dogged strength alone keeps it from being
> torn asunder.

Self-esteem is one of the most important possessions a person can
have. We often hear people wishing they had a job, clothes, car,
money, spouse or children, but seldom do you hear people talking
about self-esteem and feeling good about themselves. The best way
to solve any problem is to first admit you have one. Very few people
admit they have a low self-esteem and fewer develop strategies to
improve it. In my workshop on self-esteem, I ask the audience to give
me examples and illustrations of people portraying low self-esteem.
Listed below are frequent responses:

Young female adolescent wants a baby so she can be loved.

Students lacking confidence and assertiveness to sit in front of the
class, ask and answer questions, and participate in extra-curricular
activities.

Young male adolescents who want to hurt somebody.

Women whose major objective is to be married regardless of the
person.

Men who rape women and abuse spouses and children.

People who consciously try to alter their physical features to look
like somebody else.

People who say "you ain't nobody you black _ _ _ _ _ _ _ _"
or "niggers" ain't _ _ _ _" And probably the greatest expression
of low self-esteem is suicide.

What caused people to feel this way? What were the sources, institutions and images responsible? The University of Michigan conducted
a survey in 1950 and Motivational Educational Entertainment repeated
the survey trying to determine the major influences on children. Listed
below are its findings.

1950	Present
(1) home	(1) peer
(2) school	(2) rap
(3) church	(3) television
(4) peers	(4) home
(5) television	(5) school

The institutions have drastically changed since 1950. The peer group and the electronic media have increased their influence while school and church have rapidly declined. The home remains number one on the average, but is having serious difficulty monitoring the impact of the peer group and mass media. Let's take a look at the study and analyze each institution and its effect on self-esteem.

Home and Parents

Early-childhood research confirms the importance of parental nurturance. We know, for example, that children who are hospitalized or institutionalized in infancy fail to show normal reactions to the world about them in social behavior and even in language development. Children who are abandoned or, for other reasons, fail to receive an adequate amount of nurturance in the first years of life appear stunted in intellectual, emotional and social growth. When parents are strict, quick to punish (and slow to reward), lacking in affection and physical love expressions, their children tend to lack emotional response, appear dull and unresponsive, and perhaps, eventually to feel angry toward and resistant to any authority.

Parents affect self-esteem when they criticize the person rather than the behavior. When a parent says "*You* are a bad boy," rather than "What you *did* was bad," it has the potential to be devastating to the development of self-esteem.

I consider myself an advocate for children, not for the administrator, teacher, and parent. My major concern is that our children have a message to tell and we're not listening. Few adults listen and respect children. The major problem, both marital and in parenting, is communication. The reason is that most of us do not listen, we wait our turn to speak. This is not listening, this is thinking of what you're going to say while the other person is talking.

Child abuse can take many forms beyond the obvious physical form. There is the mental and spiritual abuse of children. There are parents who don't listen and respect their children. There are parents who want to live their lives through their children. Kahlil Gibran had these words to share in his classic book *The Prophet:*

And a woman who held a babe against her bosom said,
Speak to us of Children.
And he said:
Your children are not your children.
They are the sons and daughters of life's longing for
   itself.
They come through you but not from you,
And though they are with you yet they belong not to you.
You may give them your love but not your thoughts,
For they have their own thoughts.
You may house their bodies but not their souls,
For their souls dwell in the house of tomorrow,
   which you cannot visit, not even in your dreams.
You may strive to be like them, but seek not to make them
   like you. For life goes not backward nor tarries with
   yesterday.
You are the bows from which your children
   as living arrows are sent forth
The archer sees the mark upon the path of the infinite,
   and he bends you with His might that His arrows
   may go swift and far.
Let your bending in the archer's hand be for gladness;
For even as He loves the arrow that flies,
   so He loves also the bow that is stable.[8]

The Peer Group

The institution that now has become the greatest competitor to the family is the peer group. People have always valued the opinions and views of those people who look like them and have had similar experiences. The popular statement, "It's always good to be honored by your own" still *holds*. The peer group has risen in rank because other institutions don't take the time or have the interest or the ability to relate to young people. The peer group allows us to see ourselves in the eyes of people "who do what we do." The peer group bestows labels such as "popular" and "good looking," and this either encourages or discourages us to participate in other activities. The peer group informs its members who's "good" to date who, and whether you've qualified to participate in certain activities. When it's time to choose teams, it does not take long for you to find out what your peers think of your abilities as they begin to choose sides, nor does it take long for you to find out what your peers think about your looks and who else may be "good looking," therefore in your "league" to date. These votes of approval and disapproval are very significant to a child trying to find himself, and it becomes very difficult for other institutions to counteract their effect. Eugene Perkins comments:

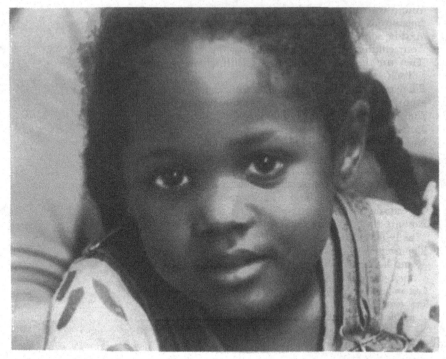

Children are extremely sensitive to the messages that are given by the people around them.

The streets constitute an institution in the same way that the church, school, and family are conceived as institutions. They all have a set of values and norms to govern and reinforce their existence. Of course, the social structure of the street lacks the sophistication these other institutions have. Nevertheless, it is an institution because it helps to shape and control behavior. And it is on the streets where the black child receives his basic orientation of life. The streets become his primary reference because other institutions have failed to provide him with the essential skills he needs to survive in the ghet-colony (ghetto-colony). And for a child to survive the ghetto colony he must undergo a rigorous apprenticeship that will enable him to compensate for the lack of guidance from other institutions and adults. He becomes a student of the "asphalt jungle" because that is where he can learn the skills he needs.

When Black children are not compelled to attend school, and often when they are, they usually can be found in the streets. The streets become their text, instructor, and subject matter. However, unlike the school, the courses in the Street Institution are structured around community norms and are more binding on its members. There are no semester breaks or summer vacations, for study in the ghetcolony is a continuous cycle which never stops, not even in the face of death.

BEHAVIORAL TRAITS OF BLACK GHETCOLONY
CHILDREN IN THE STREET INSTITUTION

Ages   Traits Learned

8 -begins to hang with small groups
-begins to learn self-defense
-begins to learn how to signify and play dozens
-knows the meaning of "p_____" and "f_____"
-has a fair understanding of his poverty
-begins to develop certain inferiority feelings about race
-begins to have certain negative attitudes toward his community
-begins to develop attitude toward school[9]

9 -becomes a better fighter
-learns about policy, craps, etc.
-begins to identify with certain specific groups
-begins occasional truancy
-becomes familiar with ghetto life styles
-begins to challenge authority models
-realizes the need to develop "coping skills"
-begins to spend more time on the streets

10 -becomes more inquisitive about sex
-becomes more acquainted with weapons
-learns how to rap
-becomes more active with groups
-begins to establish his street image
-is able to see certain ambiguities in society
-becomes more proficient with street language
-is aware of community's "hot spots"
-begins to perfect his coping skills
-begins to experiment with cigarettes and sometimes alcohol
   and dope

11 -begins associating with older boys
-begins to use the word "MF"'
-sex interest increases
-is able to distinguish youth officer, truant officer
-signifies and plays the dozen consistently
-spends most of his leisure time hanging around on street
-may have engaged in his first misdemeanor

12 -is ready for street gang activities
-has good awareness of street culture
-becomes more clothes conscious
-knows the life styles of the pimp, hustler, street man, militant,
   etc.
-can rap with adults
-may begin having sex relations
-has formed an image of himself
-may begin smoking reefers or dropping pills
-becomes skeptical of social institutions

Television and Other Media

The second greatest competitor to the home for the minds of our children is television. Many experts believe television is rapidly approaching, or has already become, number one. More information will be shared about television in the chapter on parenting; at this point we want to look at television as a form of images, and its effect on self-esteem.

Television has the power to replace imaginary, personally-created images with its own. All of our minds are filled with images of places and times and people and stories with which we've never had personal contact. In fact, when you receive information from any source that does not have pictures attached to it, you make up pictures to go with it. They are your images. You create the movie to go with the story. You hear the word "Africa" and a picture comes to mind. The question is this: Once television provides an image of these places and times, what happens to your own image? Does it give way to the TV image or do you retain it?

Neil Postman elaborates,

> Although language is heard on television, and sometimes assumes importance, it is the picture that dominates the viewer's consciousness and carries the critical meanings. To say it as simply as one can, *people watch television*. They do not read it. Nor do they much listen to it. They watch it. This is true of adults and children, intellectuals and laborers, fools and wise men. And what they watch are dynamic, constantly changing images, as many as 1,200 different ones every hour. It is an image show, a pictorgraphic medium, not a linguistic one. It is well to remember that the average length of a shot on a network television program is somewhere between three and four seconds. The average length of a shot on a commercial, between two and three seconds. This means that watching television requires instantaneous pattern-recognition, not delayed analytic decoding. It requires perception, not conception.[10]

Jerry Mander, in the *Four Arguments for the Elimination of Television*, supports Postman by adding,

> Seeing is believing. Like many an axiom, this one is literally true. Only since the ascendancy of the media has this been opened to question. Throughout the hundreds of thousands of generations of human existence, whatever we saw with our eyes was concrete and reliable. Experience was directly between us and the natural environment. Non mediated. Non processed. Not altered by other humans. The question of what is real and unreal is itself a new one, abstract and impossible to understand. The natural evolutionary design is for humans to see all things as real, since the things that we see have always been real. Seeing things on television as false and unreal is learned. It goes against nature. Yet how is a child to understand that? Western society, biased toward the objective mental mode of experience, tends to be blind not only to the

power of images, but also to the fact that we are nearly defenseless against their effect. Since we are educated and thoughtful, as we like to think, we believe we can choose among the things that will influence us. We accept fact, we reject lies. We go to the movies, we watch television, we see photographs, and as the images pour into us, we believe we can choose among those we wish to absorb and those we don't. We assume that our rational processes protect us from implantation, or brainwashing. What we fail to realize is the difference between fact and image. There is not rejection of images. Raise your eyes from the page for a moment. Look about your room. Can you reject what you are seeing?[11]

Images come from numerous sources. Television receives more attention than radio or magazines because it's a media of images, and because of the large number of hours it's watched. Children, moreso than adults, are great emulators. This is why it's so important for children to have positive role models. Images can come from direct sources such as parents and friends who may display an African identity and reflect cooperative values.

The other electronic media is radio. While not a visual medium, it too, provides or provokes images with its music. The research is not as extensive about the detrimental effects radio has on youth as television, but it's equally alarming. But we do know that the majority of the music listened to by young people is sexually suggestive, disrespectful of women, and is characterized by an increase in electronic manipulation to produce sound rather than skillful instrumentation.

The print media provides the Black community the greatest opportunity to portray Black people in positive ways. Books, newspapers, and magazines require less capital to produce than electronic media, but unfortunately they have declined in influence. The combination of deteriorating reading levels and the increased appeal of video games, television, and radio has depreciated the written word. Books are primarily used in schools; seldom are they used for recreation or entertainment. Oh, how nice were the days when you would snuggle up with a book near the fireplace and read for the evening!

A major effort by many concerned people over the past twenty years has been to improve those images our children are presented in school. Sharon Bell Mathis did a cursory review of some of the books available in public schools and libraries, and quotes from a few, among them *Durango Street* by Frank Bonham an American Library Association (ALA) notable book now in its thirteenth printing. It is the story of Rufus Henry, a Black teenager. Here are Frank Bonham's messages:

He had a small, neat Negro head and nappy hair cut short. There was a boy in one of the gangs he'd run with that they called Watusi because he was always talking about going to Africa where a Black boy could swing with anybody. An American Negro with a little education could easily take over a white tribe. Be the king of the Gold Coast! Raid other tribes and steal their gold and ivory and weapons.

Theodore Taylor, author of *The Cay* gives this message to Black children:

I saw a huge very old Negro sitting on the raft near me. He was ugly. His nose was flat and his face broad . . . His face couldn't have been blacker, or his teeth whiter. They made an alabaster trench in his mouth, and his pink-purple lips peeled back over them like meat of a conch shell . . . I knew he was West Indian.

And lastly, *Patricia Crosses Town* by Betty Baum thus:

"Why am I black mama? Is it like Carl heard from that boy in school. Am I black because I can't learn. If you're black, does it mean you're stupid?" Her father spoke, "Maybe . . . your ma's smarter than me and she is lighter than me. I never went past the third grade."[12]

A parent or teacher could have very good intentions of developing positive self-images, but not be aware of what their children are reading. The above descriptions are the exact opposite of the images needed. Richard Jones in a *Black Child Journal* article "Selecting Literature for Black Children," states,

Teachers often have a very limited understanding about how literature functions in our society, and consequently they select books for their content or didactic possibilities, or because of their availability, color illustrations and simple vocabulary. Some books are chosen because they have long been considered old favorites which all children need to read, as exemplified by Mother Goose, Dr. Seuss, Snow White and others. The indiscriminate selections of books for young Black children can have tremendous consequences, since most children's books present a world in which all the characters, at least the significant characters, are white. The message that such books carry for Black children is that do not really matter or count.[13]

Carolyn Gerald in *Black Aesthetic* confirms the importance of writer and story.

There is a tremendous responsibility being the writer. The Black child growing into adulthood through a sense of weekend movies seeing white protagonists constantly before him projecting the whole gamut of human experience, even Jesus and God are white, is persuaded that he must be white or experiences adulthood by proxy and in someone else's image. He sees a zero image of himself. The artist then is the guardian of image, the writer is the myth-maker of his people.[14]

We have discussed the various forms of media and their characteristics, but now let's look at the end result. In my workshop on images, some of the questions I ask are, What is your criteria for beauty? What is good hair? What are pretty eyes? Please note that in didactic philosophy, to know what is, is to know what is not. In other words, in order to know what is good, you must also know what is bad. In order to know what is pretty, you must also know what is ugly. Bad hair and ugly would be the exact opposite of what is good or pretty. When men and women walk past each other, value judgements of beauty are often recorded. On a 1-10 scale, with 10 representing the top of the echelon, what criteria is being used? Was it in the best interest of Black people? If America and its numerous media define beauty as light skin, long hair, fine features and any color eyes but brown as beautiful, haven't they also defined ugly? It must mean the exact opposite. It must mean dark skin, short hair, broad features, and brown eyes are ugly. In the best selling children's book, *Colors Around Us*, by Vivian Church, I show pictures of children of all different complexions. My observation has been that the pre-school and primary children applaud for all the children, while the upper-grades save their accolades for that child who best represents an European definition of beauty. Have you ever wondered about a culture where the older children become, the less self-esteem they possess?

What is good hair? I don't think anybody is more confused about hair than Black folks. We change our hair like we change our clothing. We seriously think that our hair style does not reflect our level of self-esteem. What was the political statement in the 1960's when the natural became a fad? Bebe Moore Campbell in an article in *Ebony* titled "What happened to the Afro?" explains:

> Then a funny thing happened quite predictable actually. The Afro went on sale for $29.95. Overnight it moved from a radical symbol to style with blow-out kits and wantu wazuri to keep it fashionable. In the last decade, Big Beauty (an arm of Big Business) has discovered that there's cash in kinks, or rather in straightening and curling them. An estimate on how much money Black women spend in hair care ranges from $300 to $500 million annually.[15]

The emotional cost of little girls sitting in their mama's kitchen getting burned and being unable to swim or play gym for fear of their hair "going back," are insurmountable. We must reprogram our computers, and it begins by being honest with yourself over issues like beauty, good hair, and pretty eyes. Once you admit to yourself that your criteria may not be in the best interest of yourself, your children and your people, you have made the first step. Catch yourself every time you make comments about how pretty someone is to determine what criteria you are using. Please don't delude yourself and say, "I look for beauty in the person," because study after study reports that people remain attracted initially by looks and then by personality. Secondly, find the biggest picture you can of a dark-skin man and woman with wooly hair and broad features, and just look at it over and over again until you reprogram your computer. Keep telling yourself, good hair is hair that covers your head, and good eyes are those that don't need glasses!

The School

The next major institution influencing children are the schools. We have looked at their books, but what else in the school's repertoire affects self-esteem? Teachers, principals, and general atmosphere. In the previous chapter, it was cited in a University of Chicago study of 70,000 schools that the major factor effecting student performance is teacher/parent expectations. Performance is a by-product of self-esteem and stems from high expectations. It never ceases to amaze me how most people put all public schools and their teachers in the same category. I have visited thousands of classrooms since 1974, and I continue to see a different level of expectation in each room. I can visit one classroom where the children treat me as their guest and the teacher begins to "show off" the accomplishments of the class. And yet, in the same school, I can visit another classroom where the moment I walk in, the children think it's play time, and the teacher will plead with me to speak to her children because "they really need it." I usually comply with the request for the benefit of the children, but the person who really needs it, the teacher, doesn't hear a word I'm saying. Frequent comments from these unconcerned mediocre teachers include: "You can't teach these children", and "Why should I care when the parents don't care?"

Our children are very resilient; they can respond to a variety of circumstances. For most of our children, it takes only one person to genuinely care about them for their performance to improve. Many students have responded to the coach, librarian, teacher-aide, park coordinator, and even the crossing guard. Principals are the instructional leaders for the schools, like teachers are for the classrooms. Principals and the environment they create can stimulate teachers and students to higher levels. More discussion and examples of success stories are offered in the conclusion of this book.

The Church

The last institution reported by the University of Michigan influencing children was the church. It has often been said that Black people survived slavery because of the family and the church. The comparative study between 1950 and 1992 reflects a declining influence of the church. The church in 1950 ranked third behind home and school, but now ranks last. What has happened to the church? Why do women attend church in greater numbers than men and youth? Why does Islam attract a larger percentage of men? Why was Staunton Smith Perkin's book *Satan in the Pulpit* very controversial? The full answer to all these questions would require another book probably best written by my minister and a man I truly respect, Dr. Jeremiah Wright. The two more frequent responses I hear to those questions is that the European image of Jesus and religion encourages passivity. There have been two lines of thought to counter the European image of Jesus. First, to provide an image of Jesus with African features and what is referred to in the Bible as "wooly hair and feet the color of bronze." And second, to discard the image of Jesus and focus on his works and beliefs. My optimal desire would be the second, because I have no need to express my insecurity by making every image the reflection of myself. The potential problem with no image is that the most recent image may become permanent.

The role of the church in the society, and the issue of passivity were raised by Perkins in *Satan in the Pulpit*. He charges "the Black church is the biggest rip-off in the Black community."[16] The critical mistake was one three-letter word: *the*. If he had said *some* or *the majority* of Black churches are not putting into the Black community what they receive from its members, his point would have been legitimate. But because he used the word *the*, he puts all churches in the same category. He negates and ignores all those churches historically and presently doing constructive things for the Black community. Some churches have incorporated the Lord's prayer, "on earth as it is in heaven." Young people and men want some action and programs or their attendance will continue to decline. The mistake that many people make is to write God off because of an "uneducated" minister. I sincerely believe self-esteem is greatly enhanced by putting God first. "If God be for us, who can be against us," and "greater is He in me than he is in the world." placing God first in your life should provide greater strength for struggle against oppression. The problem with many religious people is reading only half the sentence, "Love thy neighbor" — the remaining part is "as thyself." Many Black Christians love their neighbors *better* than they love themselves and submit to racism, wife abuse, and other forms of oppression.

Socio-Economic Influences

The last three areas I want to address concerning self-esteem are racism, capitalism, and sexism. It should be our objective as instructional leaders to help our children to be self actualized. I believe improving the relationship with home, peer group, television, school and church are insufficient if the effects of racism, capitalism and sexism are allowed to continue. Racism and sexism are forms of insecurity. They are a rationalization that differences create superiorities. Racism and sexism illustrate only a difference in race and sex, they do not illustrate competency. Insecure people, uncomfortable with themselves, create theories explaining their "superiority." What makes Europeans so insecure? Their lesser numbers and low levels of melanin. The majority of the world's people possess large amounts of melanin. Complete integration would greatly reduce the white European population. The dominant genes of the "majority" would greatly affect the "minority." Therefore to protect themselves, Europeans have rationalized that because they are different, they are better than people with larger amounts of melanin. What's ironic is that they will try to make people with more color feel inferior and simultaneously risk cancer darkening their own complexions. Men have done the same thing with sexism. Men are different than women, no better no worse. But men, by nurture possessing a bigger ego, have become obsessed with power. Therefore European men have created systems called white male supremacy and sexism rationalizing their superiority. People with greater levels of melanin as well as women must see through these levels of insecurities, and develop defense mechanisms. The greatest defense is the self-esteem which comes only from your culture and frame of reference.

The other remaining "ism" is capitalism, or any economy where the wealth is in the hands of the few. This system can only be maintained with the continued participation of the masses. This broad subject of economic theory is again another book; my purpose here is to look at economics only as it relates to self-esteem. Economics is a major teacher of values, the most important of which capitalism teaches is materialism. People who believe in this system, believe in its values; therefore they measure their self worth by their possessions. When I speak to young people, I put six values on the board: time, land, money, house, car, and clothes, and I ask them if they only had one choice which would they choose? The majority of the time the brothers choose cars and the sisters choose clothes. Sometimes they choose money, but when I ask them what would they buy, the answer is cars and clothes! Adults will usually answer house, but very few choose time and land.

Revolution is fought over land. All life-sustaining resources come from land. But I feel time is the most important. When you leave this earth, you will leave with clothes in the closet, car in the garage, money in the bank, house on the block, but you will leave with no more time. Unfortunately, we have allowed ourselves to be reduced to economic objects to be manipulated by the owners. There are few people in America with more time than Black folks, yet we see large numbers of men idle on corners and women watching "All My Children." We don't work unless there is money attached. The spirit to do for self, improve your skills, make something, provide a service, or return to school is connected to the dollar bill. Our self-esteem is now attached to a piece of paper. We must teach our children that education is more than reading, writing and arithmetic; but as Maulana Karenga explains in the *Theory of Kawaida* it should give a sense of "Identity, Purpose and Direction."[16] Education should teach our children who they are, because if you don't know who you are you won't know what to do with your life. If one took a random survey of high-school and college graduates, inquiring about their identity and purpose, the answers would cover a broad perspective. Their identity could include Black, Afro-American, American, minority, Bilalian, their name etc. Their purpose could be "making it," "getting over," "hanging in there," job, car, house, money, rich, etc. The most glaring example of our failure is the lack of self-esteem portrayed by our youth who lack identity, purpose and direction; seldom do we hear African-Americans as the identity, liberation as the purpose, and cooperation as the direction.

*   *   *   *   *

Presently, our children have been taught that education is needed for a job, which is the usual way to secure money. They have not been taught who they are, nor who and what oppresses them. They have been taught that school is for grades, and jobs are for money. Educators and parents of Black children must realize, as other do, that education is more than reading, writing, and arithmetic, and should also include self-esteem and values from an African perspective. My major thrust is to develop positive self-images in Black children. We have learned in this chapter the direct relationship between images and self-esteem; therefore by improving the images we enhance self-esteem. The five major institutions affecting images and self-esteem are the home, peer group, television, school, and church. It is recommended that to achieve the goal of this book we require a thorough monitoring of all five, and if possible, restoring the influence of school and church to their previous position of 1950.

The major concept I wish to highlight in this chapter in our quest to developing positive self-images in Black children is an African frame of reference. The selection of images should be based on this criteria. The parent, the primary educator of our children, should use an African frame of reference in the selection of household artifacts, wall decorations, clothing designs, entertainment, peer group, television programs, school and church selection.

The difficulty developing positive images in Black children is best manifested in our definition of beauty. Because our community has not consciously chosen an African frame of reference, then by default, we have been acculturated into accepting a European outlook on most images, and specifically the criteria of beauty. I feel the reorientation of our beauty standards is our greatest challenge in developing positive self-images in Black children. The next responsibility discussed in chapter three, "A Relevant Curriculum," will be how to maintain their curiosity and enthusiasm from the primary grades through college.

Questions/Exercises/Projects

1) What are the benefits of dark skin, wooly hair, and broad features?

2) Design a collage of an African triangle (African, Carribean, United States).

Chapter 3
A Relevant Curriculum

The relationship between curriculum, images, and discipline is of paramount importance. If an African-American child attends two years of pre-school, nine years of elementary, four years each at high-school and college, it will total nineteen years. If we multiply this with the average six-hour day, thirty-hour week, or twelve-hundred-hour year, we derive a sum of 22,800 hours. This figure is simply too large to ignore. Children spend large amounts of time in school, and how they feel about themselves can easily be determined within these 22,800 hours. If we also realize the relationship between academic achievement and economic possibilities, it may behoove us to critically assess what takes place in the classroom. Are our children being nurtured? Are they being given high expectations? Are they being encouraged to ask questions? Are they maintaining their curiosity? Are we teaching them how to think? This chapter looks at the relationship between thinking skills and high expectations, self-images and discipline.

Again, I consider myself an advocate for children. I think they have a story to tell if adults will listen. Their peer group has increased its influence for numerous reasons, but one of them is because too few adults listen and respect the ideas of children. One of my strategies to stay young and current is to view the world through the eyes of children. Children are very open, honest, innocent, and bring naive enthusiasm to an adult world that is cold, dishonest and filled with deceit. In this chapter concerned with curriculum, I feel the best place to begin is by talking to children. When I ask children, "What do your parents and teachers tell you about school?" the children respond with, "Get a good education and work hard." When I ask children how they feel about those comments, they answer, "Get a good education for *what*?" Work hard for *who*?" The children also want to know why this concept or lesson is relevant? I feel these are very good questions — what? who? and why? — and if we want to gain their trust and motivate them we must answer these questions.

The Socio-Economic Basis

Children observe adults with their "good education" and they wonder what adults end up with? A J-O-B, which they don't like consequently they end up living for "TGIF" (Thank God Its Friday). Children quickly summarize that life is about money, not a good education or a J-O-B. They also wonder why, if working hard is the solution, aren't Black people more advanced since Blacks have worked harder than anyone else in America! My response to these sentiments is provided in the diagram below:

Educated :	Trained
employer :	employee
career :	J.O.B.
think :	memorize

I believe a major problem with schools is that the curriculum is designed to *train* children rather than *educate* them. Our children do not want to be trained, and they are crying out to adults to save them. Yet, adults encourage children to go to schools without any compassion or understanding of what children are receiving in school.

John Goodlad, in one of the most exhaustive studies ever done on schools titled, *A Place Called School*, asked young people "What do you like best about school?" The students chose their friends as number one and sports were second. They could think of absolutely *nothing* as their third choice! When forced to give a fourth and fifth choice they chose their classes and teachers respectively.[1] Our children are bored to death with "this place called school." Developing positive self-images and discipline in Black children is difficult if not impossible, if they are bored, lack enthusiasm, and see no relationship between their world and the classroom.

The problems of schools, decline in student achievement and numerous related issues have been frequently discussed in all forms of media over recent years, but I feel a major problem is the increase in students who are now receiving a secondary education. In 1910, only 10 percent of the American populus received a high-school diploma, in contrast to 1992 when 85 percent of all European-Americans, 75 percent of all African-Americans, and 55 percent of all Hispanic-Americans graduated from high school.[2] These figures are even higher for those who completed some high-school years. The problem is that the economy has changed from agriculture and industrialism to post-industrialism, and now has fewer unskilled positions available. Children are now staying in school longer than they have ever stayed before, not because they like school more but because it is required.

Methods and Motivation

An industrial economy that only requires a laborer to place widget 186 on top of widget 185 for eight hours can afford to create a curriculum which trains children. But new technology requires more thinking skills and necessitates a curriculum of problem solving. Our children come to the classroom eager to learn and filled with questions, but with each passing year, children ask fewer questions and sit further in the back of the class. What is it about our pedagogy, our teaching style where the longer children are with us the more passive they become? Paulo Freire answers,

> A careful analysis of the teacher-student relationship at any level inside, or outside of school, reveals its fundamentally narrative character. This relationship involves a narrating subject (the teacher) and patient, listening objects (the student). His task is to fill the student with the contents of his narration, contents which are detached from reality, disconnected from the totality that engendered them and could give them significance. Narration leads the students to memorize mechanically the narrated content. Worse yet, it turns them into "containers," into "receptacles" to be "filled" by the teacher. The more completely he fills the receptacles, the better a teacher he is. The more meekly the receptacles permit themselves to be filled, the better students they are.

(Please note *Countering the Conspiracy to Destroy Black Boys* supports this position and explains that boys have the greatest difficulty being passive.)

> Education thus becomes an act of depositing in which the students are the depositories and the teacher is the depositor. This is the "banking" concept of education in which the scope of action allowed to the students extends only as far as receiving, filing, and storing the deposits. They do, it is true, have the opportunity to become collectors or catalogers of the things they store. But in the last analysis, it is men themselves who are filed away through the lack of creativity, transformation, and knowledge.[3]

It follows logically from the banking notion of consciousness that the educator's role is to regulate the way the world "enters into" the students. His task is to organize a process which already occurs spontaneously to "fill" the students by making deposits of information which he considers to constitute true knowledge. And since men "receive" the world as passive entities, education should make them more passive still, and adapt them to the world. The educated man is the adapted man, because he is better fit for the world. Translated into practice, this concept is well suited to the purposes of the oppressors, whose tranquility rests on how well men fit the world the oppressors have created, *and how little they question it.*

The American classroom takes on the linear style of learning.

The above banking model in contrast to the circular cognitive approach where they learn from each other.

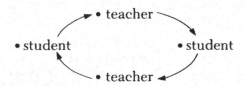

The linear model confines communication one-way, from teacher to student. In the circular model, communication flows from everyone. The linear model is static with students learning from the teacher, while the circular model is dynamic with students and teacher learning from each other.

Children and adults still learn 90 percent of what they do, 50 percent of what they see, and only 10 percent of what they hear. Yet, if you visit many American classrooms, you will either see children listening to their teachers or filling in the blanks of a workbook— which is not writing. The "fourth grade failure syndrome" referred to by numerous educators is based on the reality that from the fourth grade on, children move and talk less, questions decrease, and academic enthusiasm wanes.

Educators must remember that children want to know *why* you want them to learn that concept. Unless we answer this question, our children will not be internally motivated to learn. William Glasser in *Schools Without Failure* supports this view:

Smart children soon learn that what is important in school is one thing and what is important in life is another. We cannot assume that children know why they are in school, we must teach students the relationships of what they are learning to their lives. Our failure to do so is a major cause of failure in school. Children discover that in school they must use their brains mostly for committing facts to memory rather than expressing their interests or ideas to solve problems. Increasingly, with each passing year, thinking is less valuable than memorizing. Education does not emphasize thinking and is so memory oriented, because almost all schools are dominated by the "certainty principle." According to the certainty principle, there is a right and wrong answer to every question, the function of education is then to ensure that each student knows the right answers to a series of predetermined questions that educators have decided are important. As long as the certainty principle dominates our eductional system, we will not teach our children to think. Memory is not education, and answers are not knowledge. Certainty and memory are the enemies of thinking, destroyers of creativity and originality. It is no wonder, therefore that memorization so prized in current education leads to boredom for those who are successful and to frustration and misery for those who are not.[4]

Children are learning much of their arithmetic on a rote level. The National Assessment of Educational Progress survey of 70,000 students aged nine, thirteen and seventeen reports,

Although 60 percent of nine year-olds had correct responses on computational problems in multiplication, only 28 percent responded correctly to a word problem. The 13 year-olds performed similarly with division, 70 percent successfully completed computation problems, but only 40 percent correctly solved a word problem requiring the same skill. The assessment results clearly indicate that for most children the inability to solve word problems is not a result of their inability to compute.[5]

Searching for a way to help their students, some teachers suggest that the problem many children have stems from a reading deficiency. Considering this a real possibility, J. Dan Knifons and Boyd Holton investigated how the reading and comprehension abilities of sixth graders related to their ability to solve problems. They conducted their study with students who had made word-problem errors that were not computational mistakes. They asked individual students to read the problem aloud. Ninety-five percent were able to do so. Then they asked, "What situation is the problem describing?" Ninety-eight percent responded correctly. They followed this query by asking, "What is the problem asking you to find?" Ninety-two percent were able to answer that question. However, then they asked "How would you work this problem? Only 36 percent answered correctly. Even when students comprehended the problem, they still were unable to tell what they should do to solve it![6]

There are numerous factors effecting children's ability with word problems including comprehension and mastery of rote learning. The major problem is children do not know how to choose the correct operation to deal with the information they have. To make sense out of word problems, students need to connect the suitable arithmetic processes to the situations presented in the stories. We teach the abstract processes of arithmetic first, and then hope that the children will learn to use these processes to solve problems. That's backward and placing the cart before the horse. The emphasis on problems must come first; it's the starting place for developing arithmetic understanding and establishing the *need* for computation. The child needs to see that developing computation skills serves a purpose, that computation skills are the tools for solving problems. Arithmetic needs to be taught in a context that makes sense to the child.

Many children think that addition or subtraction or multiplication or division is when you take numbers and do something to them to get an answer. It is absurd to expect children whose arithmetic starting point has been a focus on producing answers to an isolated worksheet, and textbooks exercises to relate those experiences to search their minds for correct processes to solve word problems. Understanding the arithmetic operations has to do with recognizing the situations that call for these operations as they appear in the real world, and being able to describe these situations in the appropriate language.

Because our children have not been encouraged to ask questions, participate, and learn how to think, they have a deep fear of word problems and would prefer true/false or multiple choice. This reminds me of the study strategy I used to graduate from college. I would make up my own test questions from the professor's notes. Remember, to make up a question is to know the answer in reverse and its derivation. In my classes, I often have my students make up their own questions, incorporating the above principle.

How do we measure the success of schools? Test scores? Attendance? Reduction of crime and vandalism? Class participation? Why do children cheat? Why do teachers give tests? I feel there is an interrelationship between testing and cheating, and they are predicated on how we define success.

William Glasser comments,

Probably the school practice that most produces failure in students is grading. If there is one sacred part of education revered throughout the entire U.S. as utilitarian and necessary it is A-B-C-D-F grading. Grades are so important that they have become a substitute for education itself. Ask your own small child what is the most important objective in school and he will tell you Grades! Unless we can reduce the dominance that grades hold over our children, we will perpetuate a system in which students gradually lose necessary *internal* motivation as they gain less and less satisfaction. We depend more upon external motivates-exhortations, grades, threats, punishments, and suspension.

A team of University of Utah professors made a survey of doctors reported to American Association of Medical Colleges,

There is almost no relationship between the grades a student gets in medical school and his competence and success in medical practice. Dr. Eli Ginzberry, whose group made a similar survey of 342 graduate students who had won fellowships, found those who had graduated from college with honors were more likely to be in the lower professional performance levels.[7]

To develop positive self-images and discipline requires the encouragement of questions, thinking exercises, and a correlation between the classroom and the child's environment. It may be that in our current educational system, a student has two choices: (1) concentrate on grades and give up thinking; or (2) concentrate on thinking and give up grades and its eventual implications.

Before we move from this theoretical model of curriculum design and look at the particular learning styles of Black children, we must answer the questions from pragmatic and often frustrated teachers who may wish to "consider" the above but feel saddled by curriculum mandates from the central office. In addition, teachers and schools are currently evaluated by scores and an orderly "classroom," not the child's desire to learn and actively participate. The encouragement of movement and talking in a small classroom filled to capacity, with discipline being the major problem reported by teachers, is more than a notion.

I sincerely believe that teachers teach the way they've been taught. College education departments should provide future graduates with a "problem solving" approach to curriculum versus "banking." It is felt by many that college education departments are very conservative and often are resistant to change. Many teachers say that their college education did not equip them to teach children how to think or deal with the complexity of problems faced by inner city youth. Teachers do not teach children how to think because they don't know how. We should move away from the certainty principle and begin asking open-ended questions. I believe a major reason for teacher burnout, beyond parent apathy and poor administrative leadership, is static ideas from the linear model, in contrast to dynamic ideas from the circular model. I believe teachers, parents, and students know an awful lot about schools, but are seldom considered by administrators in curriculum design. While teachers are willing to strike over income, seldom will they organize to make the curriculum more relevant. Lastly, I believe hyperactivity comes in part from boredom; a more involved curriculum may reduce some of those discipline problems.

A major question among educators is how do children learn? Among Black educators the question frequently asked is does the present style of learning fit the mode of African-American children? The objective here is to articulate what those differences are and to encourage the advocacy of these different learning styles wherever African-American children are being taught. I feel the best way to determine the best learning style for Black children is to better understand the "capital" or "verve" that Black children bring to the classroom. Marcelle Gerber, an expert in infant testing, reports:

Comparison of African-European Psychometer Development

1) Nine hours old, being drawn up into a siting position, able to prevent the head from falling backwards (Euro 6 weeks).
2) Two days old, with head held firmly, looking at face of the examine (Euro 8 weeks).
3) Seven weeks old, supporting herself in a sitting position and watching her reflection in the mirror (Euro 20 weeks).
4) Five months old, holding herself upright (Euro 6 months) taking the round block out of its hole in the form board (Euro 11 months).
5) Five months old, standing against the mirror (Euro 9 months).
6) Seven months old, walking to the Gesell Box to look inside (Euro 15 months).
7) Eleven months old, climbing the steps along (Euro 15 months).

Contrary to social science research which labels the Black home environment as wild and chaotic because of the high activity and sound levels, Boykin contends,

Out of the Black home experience has come a unique adaptive style in Black children who possess greater psychological/behavioral verve than do their counterparts. The resultant manifestation is twofold: an increased vibrancy and an increased psychological affinity for stimulus change.[9]

The notion of vibrancy becomes even more potent when coupled with an investigation done by Yale University and University of Bridgeport researchers who found that when white children were presented with a slow paced television program, "Mr. Rogers", and then a fast paced program, "Sesame Street," the slow paced program had a more positive effect on their behavior and learning than the more "frantic" programming of Sesame Street.[10]

The above is extremely significant because Black children with greater verve are bored with "Mr. Rogers" and respond better to "Sesame Street." Unfortunately the classroom takes the pace of "Mr. Rogers" with each passing year. Na'im Akbar supports this view by adding,

> Very often, the same child who shows little or no emotion or interest in the written word can be enchanted by being read the written word. The European child will usually seek to orient himself through visual modes because this has been the conditioning of his culture. His American counterpart, with less efficient visual-motor coordination, demonstrates considerable superiority in aural-motor coordination. However, an African American child with such highly developed coordination is likely to be assessed as retarded if he is unable to demonstrate a similar facility with visual-motor coordination. Unfortunately, the IQ tests do not have a scale for measuring aural-motor activity though there are several scales which measure visual-motor activity.[11]

The above leads to speculation of the Split Brain Theory. The brain is divided into two apparently symmetrical parts. The left side of the brain is analytical, divides things into sections and specializes in the functions of math and science. The right hemisphere is more holistic, relational, and appreciates the areas of music, art, dance and sports. It has been rumored that men are better on the left and women better on the right. It has also been felt that people with greater levels of melanin are better on the right, and people with lower levels are better on the left. Are these rumors accurate? Did God go to sleep with men on the right and wake up on the left? Did God wake up for women on the right and fall back asleep on the left? Is the above phenomenon physical (nature) or political (nurture)? What can explain the tremendous rhythm of Black people and 86 percent of the starting players on NBA teams being Black, yet only 1 percent of the engineers? Hopefully the answer should be obvious: If you practice dancing and playing basketball six hours daily after school, and little time in the library or laboratory, chances are you'll be a better dancer than dentist. If Black parents and teachers emphasize one style of learning over another, if they are afraid of math and science, this will have implications on the child's development and prevent the achievement of our book title.

The major objective of a parent or teacher should be to provide educational experiences which will draw out the child's God-given talents. We must understand how children learn, that children may learn differently, and that the experiences must be diversified to avoid split brain development. Asa Hilliard has identified two styles of learning: analytical and relational. Listed below is a summary of characteristics representing both styles.

The School

As it is in general (Analytical)	As it could be (Relational)
Rules	Freedom
Standardization	Variation
Conformity	Creativity
Memory for specific facts	Memory for essence
Regularity	Novelty
Rigid order	Flexibility
"Normality"	Uniqueness
Differences equal deficits	Sameness equals oppression
Preconceive	Improvise
Precision	Approximate
Logical	Psychological
Atomistic	Global
Egocentric	Sociocentric
Convergent	Divergent
Controlled	Expressive
Meanings are universal	Meanings are contextual
Direct	Indirect
Cognitive	Affective
Linear	Patterned
Mechanical	Humanistic
Unison	Individual in group
Hierarchical	Democratic
Isolation	Integration
Deductive	Inductive
Scheduled	Targets of opportunity
Thing focused	People focused
Constant	Evolving
Sign oriented	Meaning oriented
Duty	Loyalty[12]

The question is, how do children learn? Do they have different styles? Do African-American children have a higher verve? Can the Split Brain Theory and the analytical/relational mode of learning be

Black children must develop an awareness of their historical self as well as their present self.

applied to children? What are the implications of the above to teachers and the curriculum? I think the choices are clear. We can ignore the fact that some people prefer playing with babies rather than dolls, give directions by landmarks rather than streets, prepare food by experience instead of recipe, remember faces better than names, and are motivated to learn by practicality more quickly than by theoretical abstraction. If we ignore the above, we have decided the predetermined curriculum is more important than Black children's learning style.

This chapter has attempted, first, to challenge schools to provide our children with a curriculum that will educate them by motivating thinking skills. Second, to better understand the learning styles of Black children to enhance the provision of the appropriate pedagogy or teaching style. Third, to realize that, if children are neither expected to do well nor given images of academic success, particularly in math and science, it will have a detrimental affect on self esteem. Fourth, to point out that African-American children bring a higher verve to the classroom that is being labelec hyperactive rather than being considered a challenge to a curriculum that may be irrelevant, thereby perpetuating boredom and defeating our objective of self-discipline. Lastly, to look at some recommended curriculum models.

Robert Johnson, professor at Washington University, has given considerable concern to Black participation in the sciences. In an article titled "Blacks in Science and Technology", he indicates,

> There are 355 science programs for Black students, more than 45 percent of them were aimed exclusively at the undergraduate level while only 7 percent and 18 percent were specifically targeted at the elementary and high school levles respectively. The above approaches may be viewed as short range, stop-gap measures intended to have immediate pay-offs, i.e., increased enrollment of Black students in professional and graduate schools. However, such effects do not contribute to the long term solution. The emphasis must be on long term fundamental solutions.[13]

Two institutions that I feel have done major work in the development of African-American children have created curriculum models and concentrated on the primary child are the Council of Independent Black Institutions and the Cultural Linguistic Approach Follow-Through Program in Chicago.

The Council of Independent Black Institutions (CIBI) is a national network of approximately forty Black schools, emphasizing self determination in the pre- and elementary-school level. Since their inception in 1972, teachers have collaborated on curriculum design. While more will be said about CIBI in the concluding chapter, it is mentioned here to make the reader aware of its existence, and to recommend contacting your local CIBI for curriculum strategies.

The Cultural Linguistic Approach (CLA) focuses on the culture and language of children, and views the educational process as the relationship between home and school, parent and teacher. It recognizes the parent as the first teacher and the home as the first classroom, thus culture maintains a continuous on-going role in the child's educational career. The Cultural Linguistic Approach requires teachers to recognize and accept the ethnic heritage of their students, and build the institutional program around that cultural base.

Since its commencement in the late 1960s, the CLA has been funded by the United States Department of Education for approximately 2.2 million dollars and has served over 12,000 people—children, parents, teachers and school administrators. It continues today, during these times of economic turbulence, to be at the vanguard of culture-based education. In order to implement its philosophy, the Cultural Linguistic Approach has developed an entire culture-based educational curriculum in social studies, mathematics, science, and language arts as well as an instructional methodology called USISPU. USISPU is an acronym for:

U — Unstructured Elicitation
S — Structured Elicitation
I — Interim
S — Structured Elicitation
P — Practice
U — Unstructured Elicitation

Traditional methods of teaching do not address the language and culture of African-American children. USISPU can be used for any grade level as a cultural organizational tool for teachers. It enables teachers and children to value the teaching-learning process and makes the job of teaching and learning more rewarding.[14]

Courses of Study

The subject giving teachers and parents the greatest concern is reading. The problem is not unfounded, with 42 percent of all Black seventeen-year-olds unable to read beyond a sixth grade level and the entire country possessing 23 million functional illiterates. There are numerous reasons offered for the above, including the change in the technology, family structure, decline in values, and the increase in television. All of these reasons and more can't be negated, but I agree with Rudolf Flesch that the major problem lies in the move away from phonics. A recent magazine article concurred by citing that in 1920 the basic first-grade reader had 645 different words, the 1970 reader dropped to 192, and in 1990 fell to less than a hundred. In a world becoming more technologically advanced, where parents strive to send their children to school with computers, Johnny is being exposed to fewer words than Jonathan was exposed to while on the farm. The major question that should be raised is what caused the decline? Flesch, in *Why Johnny Can't Read*, provides the answer:

> According to the basic theory of the word method, children learn to read by looking at words again and again until they know them by sight. It is therefore necessary to make them fix their eyes repeatedly on certain predetermined words. For example, during first grade a reading "teacher" decides to give them, four hundred words. He draws up a list of those four hundred words and then proceeds to write a book of "stories" containing no word outside that list and repeating each one of the four hundred words as often as possible. He then repeats the process for the second-grade reader of his series: he adds another four hundred words to the first four hundred, draws up a list of those

eight hundred words, and writes a somewhat fatter book of "stories" staying within his eight-hundred-word limit and repeating each of the eight hundred words to the utmost. Now he goes on to his third reader. Another four hundred words are added; the list now contains twelve hundred words; the book is again a little fatter and now contains the maximum variations upon the twelve hundred words.[16].

Here, for example, is the full text of a "story" called "A Funny Ridge," taken from the Scott, Foresman First Reader, *Fun With Dick and Jane.*

> Father said, "I want something. I want to get something. Something for the car. We can get it here."
>
> "Oh, Father," said Sally, "What do you want? What do you want for the car?"
>
> Father said, "You will see. You will see."
>
> UP, up went the car. "Oh, oh," said Jane. "See the car go up. The car can go for a ride. It can ride up."
>
> Sally said, "Oh! See Tim! He went up, too. He and Spot and Puff went up."
>
> Sally said, "Look, Father! Spot and Puff want to jump. Please make the care come down. Can you make it come down?"
>
> "Yes, Sally," said Father. "We can make the car come down. We will get Spot and Puff and Tim."
>
> "Look, Sally," said Dick. "See the car come down. See Tim come down. See Spot and Puff come down."
>
> Sally said, "Down comes the car. Down comes Spot. Down comes Puff. And down came Tim."
>
> "Oh, Spot," laughed Dick, "You ride up. You ride down. You ride up and down. This is a funny ride for you. A funny ride for Puff. And a funny ride for Tim."
>
> Father went to the car. He said, "The can can go. The family can go. The family can go away."
>
> "Away we go." said Sally. "We will not ride up and down. We will ride away." Away went the car. Away went the family. Away, away, away.[17]

Teachers now report that the use of books with simplified vocabulary has cut down reading difficulties in the first three grades by 75 percent. They find teaching reading a joy instead of a chore when the number of words are reduced. In other words, teaching children 1200 words in three years is a cinch. Never mind the fact that those third graders can't read a single book and are unable to decipher a single note to the milkman. Possibly, however, their figures don't look as ridiculous as they actually are. How many words should a child know when he has reached the end of the third grade? The answer to the question is immaterial when you teach reading by the phonic method. The range becomes unlimited because he can sound out any of the 44,000 words third graders have heard or said!

Books are now competing with television and the peer groups for the minds of our children; and for Black children the images of Dick and Jane, even dipped in black ink, are not enough.

Another major problem with reading is its separation from spelling and writing. The compartmentalizing approach to education does not allow for the appreciation of closely related subjects. I suggest a major goal of any reading curriculum is to ultimately have the child write his own book. It is also interesting to note how many reading experts state that four- to six-year old children are not ready to read. Numerous studies suggest that these children are capable of learning far more than "experts" are willing to acknowledge. I feel reading readiness began in pre-school when the alphabet was given. Unfortunately, it was memorized, rather than being taught that letters make sounds which together form words. The reading crisis is further complicated by the inconsistency of heavy emphasis on phonics in remedial programs, but little to no phonics in the primary division. Remedial reading teachers say it takes at least a year for children to stop guessing at words and sound out each letter. Boys, who often have a larger ego, are embarrassed learning a skill they should have learned years ago, and they often give up. Most schools incorporate phonics into a repertoire of learning strategies, but few use the complete systematic use of phonics as their *primary* source to teach reading.

History is the subject students tell me receives the "boring award." Recall how you felt about memorizing dates and events which were so far away and happened too long ago to be relevant. We must remember the major question students silently ask themselves is, why? Why do we teach history? Because it's required? Because the children need to know the origins of civilization and of this country? Why? I wonder how many concepts, lessons, and subjects would be eliminated if teachers could not prove their relevance? I believe the ultimate objective of history should be to understand the past in order to intelligently predict the future. Asking questions about when George Washington and Martin Luther King were born and when they died are static questions based on the certainty principle. The educated open-ended question is, What would Dr. King tell Jesse Jackson? I recommend, especially in the primary grades, the use of a time line to illustrate all historical points being discussed. Listed below is an example.

1929	1968	1979	**Present**	**Future**
King's birth	King's death	Student's birth		

The objective here is to illustrate that history can be touched and seen. The life of the student is a part of history. The time line also shows the continuum between the past, present and future.

Lastly, regardless of subject matter, I recommend the four creative thinking abilities, five forms of instruction, and seven levels of unity. The four creative thinking abilities according to E.P. Torrence are: "fluency, flexibility, originality and elaboration. Fluency refers to the *number* of possibilities or solutions your child can think of to any question. Flexibility refers to the *different* kinds of responses. For example, if you didn't have garden tools to dig a garden what things could you use? Originality addresses the *unusual* or uncommon solutions, and elaborates or illicits the building of stories out of basic ideas."[18]

The five forms of instruction are: written, oral, pictures, artifacts, and fine arts. The five forms are predicated on learning taking place beyond the classroom. The American curriculum relies almost exclusively on the written word in the classroom to transmit information, excluding those children who may be more receptive to an oral story, picture, field trip, artifacts, or a song, dance or drama interpretation. The use of all five forms with each concept reduces the chance of students not learning the lesson.

Maulana Karenga, in the theory of Kawaida, provides the seven levels of unity which include: self, family, community, neighborhood, nation, race, and world.[19] These levels are a set of priorities which can be used in numerous areas, of which I'm suggesting one be the curriculum. If the objective is to teach geography and appreciation of map skills, why not have a child draw a map of their room before we travel around the world? I believe the closer to the child, the more its relevancy. Teachers face the risk of losing children when the concept moves from their reality. While it is important to think in the abstract, the motivation should come from concrete experiences. Our children continue to enter our schools filled with curiosity and a desire to learn. Our challenge is to maintain and increase that curiosity and desire.

*   *   *   *   *

This chapter has looked at why the desire to ask questions, and enthusiasm for learning often decrease with age. A distinction has been made between education and training. The major hinderances to education are: the banking approach, certainty principle, grades, rote learning, and the word approach to reading. A major objective of this chapter was to better understand thinking skills and how they can be taught to children. Effective teachers must be cognizant of the child's culture and learning styles before a curriculum is designed. African-American children have a higher verve, are relational in their thought processes, and are more oral in cognition. Our ultimate quest is to develop positive self-images and discipline in Black children; this cannot be achieved if we do not include the capital of the child in the curriculum design. The failure to incorporate the above reduces self-esteem and increases hyperactivity. The next chapter on self-discipline will go into more detail.

Questions/Exercises/Projects.

1) List three questions based on the certainty principle and open-ended approach.

2) Develop two science lesson plans using both the analytical and relational method.

3) Teach your children how to make a product and provide a service that is income producing.

Discipline should be related to love and sincerity; children know who cares about them and who doesn't.

Chapter 4

Developing Self-Discipline in Black Children

1.. Begin with infancy to give the child everything he wants. In this way he will grow up to believe the world owes him a living.

2. When he picks up bad words, laugh at him. This will make him think he's cute. It will also encourage him to pick up "cuter" phrases which will blow off the top of your head later.

3. Never give any spiritual training. Wait until he is 21 and then let him "decide for himself."

4. Avoid use of the word "wrong." It may develop a guilt complex. This will condition him to believe later, when he is arrested for stealing a car, that society is against him, and he is being persecuted.

5. Pick up everything he leaves lying around—books, shoes, clothes. Do everything for him so that he will be experienced in throwing all responsibility on others.

6. Let him read any printed matter he can get his hands on. Be careful that the silverware and drinking glasses are sterilized, but let him mind feast on garbage.

7. Quarrel frequently in the presence of your children. In this way they will not be too shocked when the home is broken up later.

8. Give the child all the spending money he wants. Never let him earn his own. Why should he have things as tough as you had them?

9. Satisfy his every craving for food, drink and comfort. See that every sensual desire is gratified. Denial may lead to harmful frustration.

10. Take his part against neighbors, teachers, policemen. They are all prejudiced against your child.

11. When he gets into real trouble, apologize for youself by saying: "I never could do anything with him."

12. Never know where your child is or what he's doing when he's away from home.

13. Don't inquire into the background, personalities, records and habits of the kids he particularly pals around with.

14. Prepare for a life of grief. You'll be likely to have it.[1]

49

I used to offer the above as a humorous introduction before discussing the very serious problem of discipline. Unfortunately, I have
found many educators and parents who actually follow some of
these rules, so I now offer it both humorously and educationally.
The National Education Association (NEA) in a Gallup Poll survey
to determine the greatest classroom problem cited discipline, integration, and reading as the major problems.[2] A major contention
among educators is that time taken to discipline is time taken from
academic pursuit. Very few education departments adequately prepare teachers in the area of discipline, the area in which so much of
their time will be concentrated.

This chapter on developing self-discipline in Black children will
review numerous models, but I believe the major focus should be on
adult consistency and positive reinforcement of behavior.

Parameter of the Problem

Discipline will be analyzed both in the classroom and in the
home. While discipline has some general applications in all environments, there are also differences depending on the locale and circumstances. The child-adult ratio is higher in the classroom than at
home. The average classroom has a student-teacher ratio of 30 to 1,
versus the home with a median of 2 to 1. The above is significant in
terms of time allocation, desire for attention, and peer group influence. The increase in children reduces the individual attention
the adult can provide, but increases peer groupings.

The four major discipline problems cited by the NEA were: the
difficulty children have keeping still, resistance to being touched,
lack of respect for authority, and the love of signifying and using four
letter words. In my parents workshops, nationwide since 1974, they
have declared the lack of respect for time and property, household
responsibilites, and authority as their major problems.

To adequately address the concerns of both teachers and parents,
we must ask what the definition of discipline is and what the desired
behavior is in each setting. I advocate discipline (from the latin word
disciplus stemming from the smaller word disciple) is a system of
rules and regulations exemplified by the leader, (teacher or parent),
that motivates — not forces — followers (children) to model their
behavior. The desired behavior in the classroom is effective interaction between teacher and student, and student to student to
stimulate learning. The desired behavior at home is the willngness to
fulfill household responsibilities and to provide emotional nurturance to all members.

There are numerous reasons why discipline has increasingly become the major problem. The change in technology created a change in the economy. The move from agriculture to industrialism to post-industrialism has taken parents further from the home, spawning latch-key children and after-school programs. The above, and many more complicated issues, created high levels of divorce, changing the family structure from extended to nuclear to single. The teacher-parent relationship which used to be complementary is often viewed with cynicism and apathy. Two issues I would like to correlate to discipline are the decline in morality, spiritual training and values; and the increasing influence of television.

Behavior Influences

In the *Good News Bible*, the book of Isaiah, Chapter 3, prophesied, "The Lord will let the people be governed by immature boys. Everyone will take advantage of everyone else. Young people will not respect their elders, and worthless people will not respect their superiors." The above will result if we do not read Proverbs 22:6: "Train up a child in the way he should go and when he is old he will not depart from it." I feel the best way to develop self-discipline is by understanding and respecting God. Children are aware that parents, educators, and elders will not always notice their behavior, but if they respect and know God is omnipresent, self-discipline will prevail. I feel there is an inverse relationship between God and discipline problems; a decrease in respect for God creates an increase in behavorial problems.

The traditional values of African people have been greatly altered in America. The phrase, "When in Rome do as the Romans do" has been taken to heart by many people. Listed below is a dichotomy of values.

traditional	contemporary
African	American
We	I
cooperation	competition
internal	external

A mistake many of us make is thinking we can walk the neutral line between African and American values. Maulana Karenga states "Not to choose your culture and value system is, by default, a choice for the other culture and value system."[3] Teacher and parents teach more than reading, writing and arithmetic; they teach values.

Whatever you value, the chances are your children will value the same. Have you ever wondered why, if one student receives a high grade and another student receives a poor grade, the better student seldom offers assistance? Have you pondered why many "uneducated" parents are uncomfortable talking with "educated" teachers? I believe the answers lie in values. I feel that beyond teaching the student to excell, we have also taught the child to value "I" rather than the collective "we". It's unfortunate, but in the American value system, for many the more "educated" they are, the more arrogant and condescending they become. "Uneducated" parents may not have the Ph.D., but most have the "C.S." degree (common sense)! The child who scored a 100 should also have been taught to help those less fortunate; instead he was taught selfishness, self-preservation, and competition.

The dichotomy between internal and external values has become more pronounced with economic progress. Parents often ask, "What did I do wrong? I gave him everything." But when asked, "What exactly did you give?" the answer is usally in terms of things. Parents who want to give their children what they themselves didn't have, or want to erase their own guilt about being away for longer hours, shower children with gifts rather than time. The parents of previous generations might not have been able to buy their children stereos and cars, but they gave a lot more time. *I believe children develop better with time than with things.* I believe discipline problems have increased with the change in our values.

The other issue I propose which has greatly affected discipline is the increasing influence of television. Neil Postman in *The Disappearance of Childhood*, connects childhood to secrets. A child exposed to television is bombarded at a very early age with complicated issues that in previous generations were learned much later via the written word. The major concern lies in the reality that if children know what adults know, there are no secrets and no childhood. This problem is illustrated with children growing up much too fast, and adults acting like children. I believe children want to be disciplined, they want to know someone cares about them, they want a leader, they want to be corrected so they can learn rules and codes of behavior so *eventually* — not immediately — they can become leaders. As a result of children having to raise themselves, the following statistics have occurred. In 1950, only 170 persons under the age of fifteen were arrested for what the FBI calls serious crimes, i.e., murder, forcible rape, robbery and aggravated assault. In that same year, 94,784 persons fifteen years and older were arrested for serious crimes. This means that in 1950, adults (defined here as those over fifteen) committed serious crimes at a rate 215 times that of child crime. By 1960, adults committed serious crimes at a rate 8 times that of child crime[4]; by 1990 the rate was 5.5 times. Does this mean that adult crime is declining? No. In fact, adult crime in 1979 increased to 400,000 or 400 percent from 1950, but child crime has increased 11,000 percent!

The ambivalence between adults and children seen on television along with other factors has often produced in children a lack of respect for authority. We encourage questioning, exploration of ideas and self-expression. While these may be admirable traits, they are often encouraged too early in youngsters. The skills of knowing how to be respectful, self-expressive in a democratic manner, and how to develop independence while recognizing our interdependence are not consciously developed or taught. This reinforces my position that images and adult inconsistency have a direct relationship with children's self-discipline.

Behavior Modification Models

Educators and parents should better understand how to match their level of discipline expectations to the child's level of growth and development. Just as we don't expect the young child to think abstractly before the concrete phase has been developed, we can't expect students to be able to sacrifice — a very high level discipline skill — if they cannot listen to another person, follow directions, or work together to resolve problems of mutual concern.

Dr. Laurel Tanner in her book *Classroom Discipline* addresses this hierarchy of skills:

> What should we expect of students in grades first through third? To be able to:
> (1) listen, (2) follow instructions, (3) to share (especially the teacher's time),
> (4) to be trained in the essentials of social skills and (5) to ask questions when something is not understood.

> What should we expect of students in grades third through eight? (1) To work cooperatively with others, (2) to understand and be able to explain the reason for rules, (3) to be able to select and develop procedures for accomplishing an objective, (4) to be able to be trained as a leader and, (5) to learn the essentials of good communication skills.

> If we have done our jobs in these grades we should expect the following from our high-school students: (1) to be able to set their own schedules and time limits, (2) to work together to resolve problems, (3) to take the initiative to resolve problems of mutual concern (4) to distinguish fact from feelings and (5) to sacrifice.[5]

I believe much can be learned from the above by appreciating the stages of self-discipline. I am not affirming that some of these skills cannot be learned at earlier grades — the child's individuality and level of maturity are equally important factors — but I am suggesting consideration of this order, with time of implementation taking into account the age, personality, and maturity of the child.

In our look at the past, we should be cognizant of where discipline has been in the educational realm. A wide variety of discipline theories and approaches have bombarded the educational scene since 1960. We learned that, while physical punishment and purely mechanical behavioral systems can serve to stop disruptive behavior, they alone may do little to bring about the inner change so necessary for self-discipline to develop. We have walked our way through behavior modification, the belief that we can structure the student's environment, reward positive actions, and ignore or punish negative responses to help students behave in appropriate ways. You may have had training in communication models designed to curb discipline problems. You may also have been trained in the assertive model of very clear "I" messages. In the following pages we will look at some of these models and their theoretical and practical applications.

The first model mentioned was that of physical punishment. In my national survey of parents in workshops, I have asked them what order of discipline procedures they use with their children. The survey reveals:

1) Explanation
2) Warning
3) Isolation and/or denial of privileges
4) Physical[6]

In each discipline workshop I give, I ask parents which order they use, and the above is almost always given. My objectives with this model are, first, to provide parents an opportunity to observe what their peers are doing. Second, for them to appreciate that there are stages to discipline, and children will learn better if the stages are *separated*. I joke with parents about how some of us explain, warn, isolate and spank all at the same time! Third, the age and personality of each child may determine a different order. Some children may respond better to one order than another. Lastly, I use the model to illustrate how often what we say publicly and what we do privately are often different. Physical punishment is always last on the list — but I believe it is used far more than some are willing to admit.

Spanking used in moderation with the appropriate instrument, on the appropriate section of the body, and in the proper emotional mind-set, can be used. Please note, our objective is *self-discipline* and while spankng has "put out the fire," we still must find out and address the reason why the fire started.

The second model mentioned was the behavior modification model and its leading advocate, B.F. Skinner. The use of behavior modification can range from the simple complement for positive behavior and disregard of the negative, to complex contract negotiations and physical punishment. This technique molds selected behaviors by the types of reinforcement used and by the schedule of reinforcement.

1) When a child is rewarded, his behavior begins to change. As his behavior improves, so does his self-concept.

2) *levels of reinforcement:* generally proceed from *concrete to abstract.*

3) *common reinforcers:* food, token, points, and verbal praise. Note: concrete reinforcers are usually paired with verbal praise so that the food or token can be omitted at some point and the verbal praise will still be associated with success.

4) *choosing behaviors:* the teacher usually selects a behavior. A more mature child could be involved in this process.

5) *what to do:*
   a) *teacher selectes behavior* to be altered, i.e., child will raise his hand to request help rather than calling out.
   b) child is instructed that when he raises his hand he will receive whatever reinforcer has been chosen.
   c) child raises hand.
   d) child receives reinforcement.

6) *how to say it:* "Good, you remembered to raise you hand. Here are 2 tokens." As reinforcement progresses, we omit the second part of the sentence and simply say "Good, you raised your hand" as we place tokens on the child's desk.

7) *shaping:* it is often necessary to examine the desired behavior and separate it into parts. For example, if the desired behavior is stated: "The child will sit in a group of 8 children and attend to a 20-minute lesson," the child might first be rewarded for sitting with the group for 2 minutes, etc. until he is able to sit for 20 minutes. Then he would be rewarded each time he is attending.[7]

My objective with this model is to separate punishment, which I call stage two where the child has already broken the rule, into stage one by identifying *why* the child has not *accepted* the rule. My position is: if we can get the child to accept the rule in stage one, punishment or consequences will be reduced. My workshop participants have provided numerous reasons for the lack of acceptance. They include adult inconsistency, lack of communication, lack of child's input, perceived unfairness, lack of enforcement, declining respect for God, peer pressure, and mass media. While most of these are self explanatory, let me describe a few in more detail. A major reason for lack of acceptance is adult inconsistency. A teacher in 201 may have one rule and the teacher in 203 will have another. Mother will have one rule and father will have another. A parent will have one rule on Monday and another on Wednesday. Lastly, adults continue to say, "Don't do as I do, but do as I say." If the objective is self-discipline, adults must become consistent leaders.

The lack of communication occurs in two areas: explanation and understanding. Self-discipline cannot occur with statements such as, "Do it because I said do it." An explanation of why and its consequences is necessary in order for the child to follow the rule outside the presence of an authority figure. Further, adults must be sure the child understands the rule by listening to the child's interpretation of the rule and its consequences. The major problem in communication lies here because few of us *listen*, most of us are thinking about what we're going to say when the other person is talking.

I believe children should have *input* in the rules that govern their lives. I did not say they should *determine* the rule, but if the objective is self-discipline and not a dictatorial model, their input is needed. Finally, another reason given for non-acceptance is lack of enforcement. Children often tell me they are given eight commands from their mother to empty the garbage and two from their father! Children know from the tone of voice or other indicators when you will back up your command. They also are perceptive enough to know adults often are inconsistent with their rules and the consequence of their infraction.

My use of the broad behavior modification range is based on one word: *attention*. I believe a major reason for discipline lies in the fact that children crave attention and have found only two ways it can be secured. Children can either do something good and *maybe* receive *praise*, or do something bad and almost always receive *criticism*. A classroom example: Thirty children with twenty-eight acting very good and two behaving negatively will result in attention given to which group? When the two begin to act correctly, will they get more attention then they got from their negative behavior? Unfortunately, the answer is no. I believe there is a direct correlation between self-esteem and praise, both in the giver and the receiver. In order to praise someone, you first have to feel good about yourself. You have to understand that a complement given about someone else does not lessen your accomplishments. In a world filled with racism, capitalism, sexism, non acceptance of God, lack of historical pride, competition, and conditional love from parents, few of us are secure enough to praise others. Children demand attention and have shown they will do anything for it. They have found this precious commodity is forthcoming much faster with negative behavior than with positive behavior. A child acting correctly is often overlooked and becomes part of the status quo. A workshop presenter in Ohio believed that to produce a child with a healthy sense of self-esteem and self-discipline requires a ratio of five parts praise to one part criticism. I was shocked because presently the ratio is exactly the opposite; children are criticized far more than they are praised. Originally, I was hoping to just improve the ratio to equality, but I now realize we have a lot more work to do to achieve the five-to-one ratio.

The behavior modification approach is predicated on identifying what the child values, and correlating that with positive behavior. I believe children want attention, and will either perform positively or negatively depending on which will give them the greatest amount of attention.

The next model we shall look at is the communication model. The objective here is to connect behavior with articulation. The child should be able to describe and analyze his or her own behavior. Self-discipline is predicated on the child being able to know the difference between right and wrong. The communication model can exist between any number of parties, from the one-on-one parent-child or teacher-student to the larger group model. Described below is the peer-group version of communication. Studies show the tremendous influence of the peer group on children; this group can either influence children positively or negatively. The objective of this peer-group session titled Unity/Criticism/Unity (U/C/U) is to take the burden of disciplining off the adult and place it on the peer group. The method that follows can be used with all age groups and with any number, ranging from the family structure to office and classroom. The example below will be taken from the classroom. We believe that when a problem arises, honest, direct, open communication between those involved should take place. If a resolution cannot be achieved, it is taken to the entire group.

(A) All the children form a Unity Circle. Rationale: Environment plays an important part in effecting behavior. Since we come together to help one another because we care for one another, a Unity Circle is most desirable.

(B) The coordinator or teacher of the session opens by saying, "Are there any words of praise?" Rationale: We come together to teach children how to find beauty in each other, complement and reward good behavior. This is especially satisfying to a child who was criticized during the last session but who has modified his or her behavior to the benefit of the collective.

(C) The teacher then asks, "Are there any criticisms?" In response to the teacher's question, the children raise their hands. This is done in an orderly manner. Any child who has an emotional outburst loses the chance for making a criticism. The teacher then records all hands raised. The role of the teacher is to coordinate, i.e. to make sure rules are followed, but not to take the disciplining of the child away from the collective. Rationale: We want to develop our children into logically thinking adults. We therefore expect a conversation which will not be filled with shouting and words of anger. We also wish to avoid criticism being given in reaction to a criticism placed upon someone. Our structure prevents the negative reaction of, "Since you criticized me I'm going to criticize you" from occurring. Criticisms are required to be given in a constructive way. We do not want children destroying each other. Only those children who have raised their hands are eligible to give criticism. Please also note that the children, so far, have only expressed that they have criticisms to give, but have not yet given it.

(D) The teacher then goes around the room to those who had raised their hands, seeking the nature of their concern. Again, any child who has an emotional outburst loses the chance to criticize. Rationale: We are trying to teach the children to communicate, to clearly express themselves. We also want a session where we think before we speak. By asking only for criticism at this time, the child who is being criticized has to think about it to himself or herself until we later ask for responses. We find that the immediate reaction to a criticism is defensive. We try to avoid that reaction by having some time elapse so that the child has to deal with it first before responding. A child who is being criticized and who speaks immediately in anger is also criticized for that, and sanctions are established, such as having the child write on paper the reason why he or she cannot control their temper, or having a letter sent home to the parent requesting a visit.

(E) The teacher will then ask the child who received the criticism, "What are your feelings about it?" The child answers by saying, "My feelings are . . ." A dialogue may develop between the two children.

This must be orderly. No other children can speak without teacher approval. Other children must also have pertinent information to provide. A child entering a discussion simply for the sake of the discussion can also be criticized. When the dialogue has ended, if action is then needed, the teacher will ask the class what they feel the punishment should be. A majority is needed in any sanctions. Teachers must make sure that the sanction is fair. This is done in the form of suggestions. Rationale: The restriction of who can enter into the discussion forces clarification of the issues. Teachers should moderate with this as the basic goal. Political science is taught through the voting procedure. Children feel the sanction is fair and correct when it comes from their peers. We find peer group pressure is much stricter than the pressure from teacher to child. Teachers should be cognizant of group members operating "behind the scene."

(F) At the completion of the UCU session we stand up in our Unity Circle and, through the creativity of the teacher, a form of unity through song, chant, etc. is expressed.[8]

I have found U/C/U works better with younger children but is needed more by older students and adults. In our society, unfortunately, the older many of us become, the less open and honest we become. Pre-school and primary-grade children say exactly what they feel, making for a very productive session. Older students and adults often say what they feel only behind a person's back, avoiding wholesome dialogue. Hopefully, if young children are brought up with the U/C/U model, this malicious behavior will not be manifested in later years.

The communication model can only be productive if we know how to criticize. Too often we criticize the person rather than the behavior. The person being criticized will become defensive of his or her person, but may be more open to criticism of his or her behavior. African, Chinese and Japanese cultures are tremendously different from Euro-American culture in this respect; the former cultures are aware of the personhood, soul, spirit. If a child or adult has done wrong, great care and pain is taken to thoroughly review the behavior without tarnishing their self-esteem. The Euro-American culture, predicated on values exhorting "I" and competition, often can be found "taking someone over the carpet signifying, gossiping, and playing one-upmanship" with each other. I believe another problem with communication, besides inattentive listening, is the desire to debate and argue rather than to engage in harmonious discussion.

Frequent questions asked about U/C/U concern the modes of punishment and the time allocated. The goal of the session is to allow the children to determine the punishment because children respect it more when it comes from their peers—and usually it's more strict. The coordinator or judge should only step in if the punishment is deemed unfair. If the children determine a child should be burned at the stake, the coordinator should recommend less severe measures! Coordinators may want to provide a list of disciplining actions for the group to choose from at the beginning of the year.

It is recommended that U/C/U take only fifteen minutes each day. The importance of the session is that it takes place each day, and children will know that if they do anything wrong, subsequently they're going before their peers. Just as in court, there will be days when you will have a backlog and you will have to address those cases the following day; but every effort should be made to keep the consequence close to the behavior. Ideally, you will reach a point where the session will be filled with praise, few or no criticisms, and followed by chants and songs.

The last discipline model I want to look at is the assertive model, or, as I call it, the Tight Rope Theory! When I was younger, I used to believe the best disciplinarians of Black children were Black men, followed by Black women, white men, and lastly white women. I believed this until I observed a Chicago public school, fourth grade classroom instructed by a Black man. We had to begin hollering to each other because the noise level from the children had become so high. What I've noticed about children is that they feel compelled to find out how far they can take you on your "rope." In this class they had to go over the edge before this man finally responded.

Later in that year, in a Los Angeles public school, I met a sixty-two year old European teacher teaching seventh grade Black children. This teacher decided years ago that she was there to teach, not to holler and run around chasing children. When a child drops a pen, she looks at the child, then the pen, and before she looks at the child again the child has picked up the pen and resumed his or her work. This teacher's "rope" is not only tight, it is consistent. Some teachers can be taken to different points on their ropes on different days. Children feel obligated each day to find out where they can go on your rope. I have been told that the teacher in Los Angeles has been responding at the same point for the past thirty-two years, and even the children have stopped trying to find the point on her rope! I have changed my views on who can discipline Black children, just as

I believe a Chinese teacher can teach a Russian child mathematics. But I still believe that only a Black teacher can teach a Black child an African frame of reference.

Assertive Discipline is a competency-based approach to discipline which has been utilized by over 300,000 educators in public and parochial schools nationwide. Educators report that Assertive Discipline has enabled them to reduce behavior problems by 80 percent. Assertive teachers take the following stand in the classrooms: I will tolerate no student's stopping me from teaching. I will tolerate no student's preventing another student from learning. I will tolerate no student's engaging in any behavior that is not in his or her own best interest and in the best interests of others. And most important, whenever a student chooses to behave appropriately, I will immediately recognize and reinforce that behavior. Finally, assertive teachers are the bosses in their classrooms. They have the skills and confidence to take charge.

Lee Canter, the author of *Assertive Discipline* focused on what types of teachers do not respond effectively to student behavior.

We labeled such teachers either nonassertive or hostile. Nonassertive teachers do not clearly or firmly communicate their wants and needs to the students or if they do, they are not prepared to back up their words with actions. They are passive or wishy-washy with students and lack the skills and confidence necessary to deal effectively with disruptive behavior. Hostile teachers, on the other hand, get students to do what they want, but in so doing they violate the best interests of the students. These teachers often verbally or physically abuse students.

The following example shows how each of these three types of teachers would deal with a student's disruptive behavior. Suppose the teacher wants the children to do their work without talking or disrupting the class. During the work period, one boy puts his work aside and begins to talk loudly to the children around him. What should the teacher do? In such a situation, the nonassertive teacher would, typically, walk up to the boy and ask him to get to work. When he doesn't, teacher shrugs and says, "I just don't know what to do with you!" The hostile teacher would, typically, storm up to the boy and yell, "You have the biggest mouth I've ever seen. Shut it or you'll be sorry!" But the assertive teacher would, typically, walk up to the boy, look him in the eye, and tell him firmly "Stop talking and get to work now. If you don't you will have to finish your work during free time."

For teachers to become more assertive and thus more effective in dealing with behavior problems, they need skills. The following are the competency skill guidelines teachers should follow to deal assertively with student behavior: The teacher must know at all times what he or she want students to do. Typical behavior teachers want from students includes following directions; staying in their seats, raising their hands when they want to speak; getting to class on time; keeping hand, feet and objects to themselves; bringing pencils, books, and paper to class. The teacher must communicate these wants to students both verbally and visually, i.e. post rules. The teacher must know how to systematically set limits when students do not behave properly. The teacher must know how to systematically reinforce the appropriate behavior to students.

The teacher must know how to elicit the cooperation of the principal and parents in the discipline efforts with problem students. Many parochial schools have thus arranged to train parents in the same basic Assertive Discipline skills they utilized with students. Parents must assertively take charge when their children misbehave in school. Many parents of problem children are reluctant to assert their parental authority firmly. Parents must be taught that they need to deliver a firm, clear message to their children: "I will not tolerate your misbehavior at school!" Parents must be taught that for their children's and their own best interest, they need to be in charge and that it is O.K. to demand that their children behave.[9]

As mentioned earlier, teachers rank discipline as the major classroom problem, exceeding both integration and reading. The problem is clearly evident when you visit middle and high schools that appear more like fortresses than schools. These efforts were deemed necessary not only to ward off the negative influences from the outside, but to better contain those on the inside. Recently, in a Detroit private school, a child was accidentally killed by another child who was showing off a gun he had brought for "protection." A Chicago public high school recently experienced a shoot-out in the cafeteria where three students were wounded. An academic environment is greatly hampered when everyone is walking around ducking bullets. I empathize with police and school superintendents who attempt to provide a systematic structure to the intricate problems of discipline. These efforts, while well intended, are too distant from the child to develop self-discipline. These programs are one step away from the juvenile courts and prisons that seldom rehabiliate, but more often perpetuate repeat offenders.

Provided below is an excerpt of Chicago's Uniform Discipline Code. These codes have become necessary because of adult inconsistency, little attention to positive behavior, parental apathy, lower teacher expectations, declining respect for morality, increasing influence of the mass media, and poor communication.

1. **Teacher-Student Conference**
   The teacher shall talk to the student and they shall mutually agree upon and sign a statement of expected student behavior. Copy of statement is maintained in teacher's file.

2. **Teacher-Student-Parent Conference**
   The teacher, student, and parent(s) mutually agree upon and sign a state-

ment of acceptable student behavior in a formal conference. Copy of statement is maintained in teacher's file.

3. **Teacher-Student-Parent-Resource Personnel and/or Administrator**
A formal conference is held to plan for corrective counseling, referral to outside agencies, or other appropriate actions. Record of action taken shall be signed by all parties and maintained in administrator's file.

4. **In-School Suspension**
The student remains in school. All privileges are suspended; classes are not attended. Action is recorded in student folder.

5. **Disciplinary-Reassignment**
Disciplinary action can include transfer to another room as a regular or alternative school placement for a specifice period of time. Action is recorded in student folder.

6. **Suspension (one to five days)**
The student is informed regarding the due process procedure. Parent is notified of student's suspension and is informed of the due process procedure. Action is recorded in student folder.

7. **Suspension (six to ten days)**
The student is informed that he/she is suspended and is informed regarding the due process procedure. Parent is notified of student's suspension and is informed of the due process procedure. Action is recorded in student folder.

8. **Police Notification**
An incident report is filed with the Police Department. Action is recorded in student folder.

9. **Arrest**
A complaint is filed by the school police.

10. **Expulsion**
The student and parent are informed by registered or certified mail for a hearing for the purpose of expulsion through the due process procedures.[10].

The strength of these codes is its attempt to systematize and bring consistency to all its employees in the manner in which they address discipline problems. Secondly, the codes mandate communication at the first three levels. Unfortunately sytems can't make people consistent, complementary, compassionate, open, and honest in their dialogue. Thirdly, there has been an attempt to avoid outside suspension — which some children actually wanted — by creating in-school suspension. These suspensions, while illustrating the severity of the problem to the student, keep the students off the streets and able to stay abreast of their class studies. Lastly, as mentioned previously, the codes are a band-aid approach responding to years of parental and teacher neglect.

In conclusion, our objective is to develop self-discipline in Black children. I believe consistent adults who reinforce positive behavior can achieve this goal. The four major types of discipline problems are: students' hyperactivity, resistance to being touched, the lack of respect for authority, and the habit of signifying and using four letter words. I have attempted to look at the larger issues causing disciplinary problems and models that may correct it. With the above in mind, let's look again at each problem.

Hyperactivity may also occur because they are bored with a passive, irrelevant curriculum (cited in the previous chapter) that denies movement and student participation. The encouragement of movement and increased responsiveness to hyperactive students can better utilize this high energy level which may be due to the large intake of sugar in their diets. Many children start off the day with sugar cereal, Hostess Twinkie, candy bar, or pop. If you visit most classrooms and monitor the energy level you will see highs and lows directly related to their meal schedule. Lastly, the students' difficulty being still may be because he has not been taught.

The resistance to being touched and the fights starting because of children brushing up against each other may very well cover a deeper issue. In a society based on independence, few of us are strong enough to admit that we need each other, or admit when we're emotionally hurting. Males have the greatest difficulty expressing intimacy and the need to touch. The resistance to being touched may be due to the fact they have not been touched and given enough attention. Oftentimes, adults may be able to avert a discipline problem by hugging a child. Unfortunately, many children are only touched in anger; we must correct this practice.

The lack of respect for authority may lie not only in our earlier analysis of adult inconsistency, but also in the lack of respect adults have for themselves. I still hear a few adults tell me that when they walk by a group of youngsters, they improve their conversation. It's amazing how youths can be near some adults and talk one way, and then converse much differently around others. It illustrates how adaptable and resilient children can be depending on the circumstances. They can be disciplined in one moment and outright rowdy in another. Adults must neither be afraid of children nor buddy-buddy; they must be leaders. The accelerated childhood described by Neil Postman has made the adult-child relationship very ambiguous. Adults must be keenly aware of the distinctions.

The desire to signify, play the dozens, and use four-letter words illustrates the values of the American society of "I" versus "we." When a child receives a grade of 100 and another receives 40, the present value system does not encourage support for the lower achieving student, but condemnation. There remains only two ways to "be somebody" lift yourself up, which demands work; or tear someone down, which only requires talk. Insecure people feel better when they tear people down because they are unable to praise. Our children didn't come into this world playing the dozens, they learned from their parents and peers. We must develop self esteem and teach children how to praise and complement.

Finally, I believe discipline is related to love and sincerity. Children know who cares about them and who doesn't. They know when rules are made for their benefit and when rules are made for adults. Children now live in a society where some teachers and parents do not love and care for them. Some teachers now teach because they cannot find a job elsewhere. Some parents had children irresponsibly, and they themselves have low self-esteem. The inter-relationship between self-esteem, consistency, complementary, assertive, adult role models are the ingredients necessary to achieve the objective of this chapter. The historical solution to discipline problems, like so many other problems, has erroneously been answered with one narrow, isolated approach. The answer to discipline problems is not the selection between spanking and consultation, but a holistic approach appreciating the virtues of each model. This chapter has attempted to provide a review of each model with the accentuation on consistency, praise, and assertiveness in each of them.

*   *   *   *   *

Our overall desire is to develop positive self-images and discipline in Black children. We have looked at the hindering factors, the need to develop an African frame of reference in selecting images, the promotion of thinking skills that maintain curiosity and the enthusiasm to learn, and, in this chapter, the need for consistency and praise to develop self-discipline. The next chapter takes a specific look at how parents can develop positive self-images and discipline in Black children.

Questions/Exercises/Projects

1) Develop a chart, and, for a week, monitor the number of praises and criticisms.

2) Conduct a U/C/U session at home and/or in the classroom.

Parents need to feel good about themselves before they can truly transplant this feeling to their children.

Chapter 5
Parenting: Children Are The Reward of Life

The developing of positive self-images and discipline in Black children starts with the acceptance that parents are the first and primary educators. The parent-child relationship starts with prenatal care, and often can be found still working positively or negatively in adulthood. One of my favorite workshops is the one for parents titled "Children Are the Reward of Life." What follows are many of the ideas discussed in that workshop.

One place to see what America values, is in what their schools teach. If you want to be an engineer, doctor, accountant etc., there are schools for that; but if you want to be a father, mother, husband, or wife there are few, if any, schools. The importance of child rearing and marriage is left to guesswork, trial and error, and whatever you picked up from your parents. The values and priorities in America emphasize career and money, not family stability. Ironically, most employers admit the tremendous loss of employee productivity due to family problems. This chapter is an attempt to formalize the parenting process to encourage more workshops, seminars, courses, and books on what I feel is a very worthwhile subject.

Home and Family Importance

The values of American society have followed the changes in economy, which has moved from agriculture to industrialism to post-industrialism. The family has responded with movement from extended to nuclear to single parenting. If, initially, the desire for children was for their income, that economy has ended. The greater participation of women in the marketplace, and their desire for career achievement has also lessened the desire for children. The move of the population to greater than 80 percent urban has further reduced the desire for children. The availability of birth control pills has reduced the number of children without a decrease in sexual activity. The only element of our society encouraging the birth of children are archaic welfare laws that encourage irresponsibility, prompt men to leave their families, and create dependency.

Few adults have peers encouraging pregnancy. You often hear complaints about the tremendous sacrifices necessary after having children—giving up a new pair of shoes, evening entertainment, and classes for career advancement. I strongly believe that if you can't list at least five *joys* you receive from your children right now, that may be the reason why your job seemed so hard. You've been experiencing the denials and not receiving the joys. Where are you going to find—at Sears, K-Mart, or your local disco—a four-year-old child who wants to be grown, yet, when it's time to go to bed, requests, child-like, that you keep the light on? Where are you going to find anything equal to a child who runs into the kitchen, holds you by the leg, and says, "I just wanted to be close to you." Where are you going to find anywhere in your career, a child who is now an adult who calls—not just on your birthday, father or mother's day—and says, "I just wanted to say thanks for all you've done for me." If you truly want to appreciate one of the "seven wonders" of the world, look into the eyes of a child. They will show you a view of a world filled with innocence and innate possibility.

One of the major objectives of my workshops and this chapter is to reflect on a study of major influences on children previously cited by the University of Michigan.

1950	**Present**
1. home	1. peer
2. school	2. rap
3. church	3. television
4. peers	4. home
5. television	5. school

Major changes have occurred since 1950. Many of us have been operating with "the good old days" mentality in this rapidly changing era. Home, school, and church have been losing to the peer group and television for the minds of our children. I advocate the way to develop positive self-images and discipline is to, first, be informed. Once the problem has been identified, parents should consciously work on returning their family lifestyle to that of the 1950 study. First, quantitatively, ask yourself about your child's sixteen waking hours. How much time do they presently spend in each of the above five listed areas? Second, qualitatively, identify all the issues your children talk about, i.e., movies, music, sports, clothes, money, television shows, entertainment, sex, drugs, etc. Ask yourself who influences your child on these issues. The honest answers to these questions will give you a realistic assessment of what must be done.

The peer group and television have begun to raise our children. I recommend a *parent's home program.* There are two distinct parts of a child's day: nine to three, when they're in school; and three to nine, when they're at home. Parents often want to know what teachers instruct between nine and three, but where are the parent's lesson plans from three to nine? The major complaint I hear from teachers is the increasing burden that parents place on them. Parents can start their involvement by asking the appropriate question. If you ask *how* was school today, you've asked an evaluative question. Children quickly respond with, "It was alright", "Okay", or "Fine". If you ask your child, "*What* did you do in school today?" you've asked a descriptive question. Children are forced to remember what happened from early in the morning until late in the afternoon. They begin to learn good communication skills versus one-word answers. Children also know from your questions how much time, love and attention you want to give them.

Parent Involvement

In addition to asking your child what he/she did in school, I suggest you ask the child's teacher and principal what they did also. Something strange has happened in schools; parents, who are owners of the school because they are taxpayers, have forfeited their powers to teachers and adminstrators. Today, these two groups often look at parents with a "what-are-you-doing-here" attitude. The relationship between teachers and parents needs to be strengthened. The academic success of children is dependent on high expectations and cooperation between parent, teacher, adminstrator, and student. A workshop presenter in Chicago believes parents can be divided into two categories when their child's lack of progress is being discussed. The first group will provide personal circumstances that have contributed to the child's poor behavior. The second group will simply say, "Thank you for informing me, you won't have any more problems."

It's unfortunate, but as the child's age increases, parents' involvement decreases. When I speak to Headstart parents' groups, about 75 percent are in attendance, elementary 30 percent, and high-school meetings rarely exist because of the sparse attendance. One of the excellent components of Headstart is its mandate for parent involvement. Title I had this same mandate, but with revised legislation it became Chapter I, and parent involvement became optional. Often, graduating Headstart parents want to remain involved, but I seriously doubt whether elementary schools know what to do with parents. Imagine thirty parents going to the principal's office saying they came to volunteer. The distinction should also be made between involvement and support. A fair evaluation of parents should go beyond who participated in the bake sale, but should also include the complementary reinforcement parents give teachers at home.

Schools often have to use "gimmicks" to secure parents involvement, including report cards, children's assembly programs, door prizes, and food. Schools teach parents the way they teach children, using Frieres "banking approach". They determine for parents what they should know. My experience has taught me that with the changing demographics of today's parents, workshops on parenting should come after workshops on self-esteem, beauty tips, male-female relationships, career development and communication. We have some parents who need to feel good about themselves before they can transplant this to their children. These workshops should be followed by sessions on peer group management, discipline, television, and single parenting.

The problem is magnified because teachers have not been taught parent interaction skills. In our society, we often find that the more degrees and money a person has the more arrogant and condescending they are. Parents are often uncomfortable talking with teachers and administrators because they don't know what to say or how it will sound. I have noticed that those schools that have adequate parent involvement go beyond sending out a thousand fliers, but have a parent coordinator, and staff and principal who have established a personal rapport. Parents, like children, know when they're welcomed. All teachers must appreciate the cultural background of African-American parents.

I do not want to appear biased toward parents; schools are not the only reason for lack of involvement and support. Many parents simply place the burden of education on the staff. Private-school parents are just as guilty, often expressing their commitment only through their checkbook. The tremendous increase in discipline and

Black children being placed in special education classes — educable mentally retarded and behavior disorder — is also related to the breakdown in the parent-teacher relationship.

I never compare public and private schools because of the numerous differences, including tuition, lower student-teacher ratio, and the ability to remove teachers and students who do not enhance the educational environment. Public schools must educate everybody, including children who are now raising themselves. Studies have shown that public schools do an adequate job educating students where there is parent support, but do very poor where it is lacking. Public schools cannot fill the void of the home. What follows is a home program to complement the school curriculum. The major ingredient of the home program is time. Many parents say they gave their children everything, but when asked for details, their answers are things, not time. We do not have eighteen years to develop our children; we have six hours a day on weekdays, sixteen hours on weekends, plus summers, multiplied by eighteen years, which equals only seven years and 313 days.

We should view our children the way a coach views his team or a farmer views his crops. What can I do to make my team, crop or child better? I believe parents control the *process*, not the *result*. Parents cannot determine for certain how a child will grow, but they can determine the stimuli and experiences that can enhance their growth. All children have been given talents by God. Unfortunately, many children grow up and never develop these talents. The universal law is: You lose it, if you don't use it. A major objective of parents should be to provide as many diversified experiences as possible to find their child's talents.

Time management has direct application to organizational skills. A frequent complaint from teachers is the disorganization of their students. Many students have difficulty taking care of their note books, desk, and other responsibilities. A cursory look at the home provides very good clues on where this behavior is manifested. Schools establish a daily routine that is seldom seen at home. Children often eat, sleep, do their homework, watch television, play outside, and do their chores whenever they choose. Schools are appealing to parents to establish a routine with their children. Mothers may pick-up after their children, but teachers do not feel that's part of their job.

Some parents, unlike coaches and farmers, have forfeited their home program to the peer group and television. The parenting process starts and ends with, "Play outside" or "Go watch T.V.," the very institutions that have detrimental effects on the goals of this book. The reason for this attitude are numerous and complex, ranging from the changing economy and family structure, to declining emphasis on morality and internal development to materialism and external development. Parents don't have the time or the priority to design a home program. The home program I'm recommending should be on a schedule. It should include the dinner, bathing, sleeping hours, homework, Black culture, monitored television, spiritual activities, outside entertainment, skill development, outside play, home games, good communication where listening is emphasized, consistent discipline versus inconsistent punishment, family field trips, library, nutrition, sex education, household responsibilities, high expectations, and lots of affection. There is no way of insuring that children, with this home program, will grow to be responsible, self-actualized adults, unashamedly Black and religious; but you will sleep good every night knowing you control the home program, and the children control the results. Of course, I know children and adults make their decisions based on their experiences, and that's my home program.

I believe that if the family can only control one hour, it should be the dinner hour. The American lifestyle has turned the house from a home to a transit station. Meals are often eaten while passing through. Family members walk into the kitchen and grab a plate. The present trend of both parents working has brought up the issue of who is responsible for meal preparation. Families often use the criteria: first one home. If the traditional role structure of women cooking or the above criteria are not in effect, they probably eat out. Single parents, while not complicated with the role of the other partner, could also do better by having all family members eating dinner together.

Role of Nutrition

Parents should also be concerned about *what* they feed their children. Nutrition is a very important component of the home program. How can we develop Black children who feel good *about* themselves when they *do not* feel good? Very few Americans have been taught proper nutrition. Science curriculum often provide a more thorough analysis of the planets than good nutrition. Medical schools are equally blatant in their low regard of nutrition. Common illnesses like arthritis, rheumatism, hypertension, heart disease, and cancer are related to poor nutrition. These problems are multiplied by a medical profession and a society that prefers responding to the symptom rather than prevention. Doctors in America get paid when you're ill, but in China, doctors get paid when their clients are well. (A monthly fee is paid to doctors when you're well as an incentive for doctors to maintain this state. The fee is not paid when the patient visits the doctor).

I don't expect proper nutrition to be sponsored by the cattlemen's association or the dairy council. This prostituted form of research is what is generally taught to our students. Many problems occur when the natural product has been processed and bleached: white sugar, flour, bread, rice, and noodles are prime examples. Parents could provide the missing nutrients by simply substituting the above with brown sugar, honey, wheat or rye flour, bread, brown rice, and wheat noodles. The number-one cited discipline problem is the difficulty children have in being still, or hyperactivity. A nutritional cure to this problem could be the reduction of sugar in the diet. Many children start off the day with a Hostess Twinkie and a bottle of pop. The use of sea salt rather than land salt, monitoring fried food, and eliminating pork will greatly reduce hypertension, a major killer in the Black community.

Since 1930, little girls have started their menstrual cycle six months earlier for every decade. Young girls are now starting their menstrual cycle as early as eight years of age![1] The reasons for this are complex, but the major reason is the increased protein in the diet. Every mother in the animal kingdom has *the* appropriate milk for *their* offspring. Dogs feed their puppies, cats feed their kittens, cows feed their calves, but man, the most sophisticated animal, sends its babies to another animal for milk. Cow's milk develops the body; breast milk develops the brain.

The most important period of a child's learning or conceptual development is not years three to six as many child psychologists and learning theorists advance. It is far more critical than that. The most important period of a child's learning is from conception to year six. To be more exact, the period of most rapid brain growth is between the fourth month of pregnancy and the sixth month after birth. By the end of the child's first year, the brain has achieved some 70 percent of its adult weight, and has practically completed its growth by the end of the second year.[2]

Prenatal and postnatal nutrition are essential. Generally the consequences of nutrient deprivation are:

1) The brain has fewer cells.

2) the myelin sheath which insulates nerve cell and speeds nerve impulses, has abnormal formation.

3) There is faulty enzyme development.

4) There are fewer nerve connections in the nervous system.

5) There are lower amounts of some nerve hormones.[3]

To illustrate how far from the ideal cow's milk is to human's milk are some comparisions.

	Human	Cow
Protein-total %	1.0 to 1.5	3.5 to 4.0
casein %	50	82
whey %	60	18
Calcium-phosphoric ratio	2:1	1.2:1
Vitamin A (unit B per liter)	1898	1025
Niacin (mg. per liter)	1470	940
Vitamin C (mg. per liter)	43	11
reaction in the body	alkaline	acid[4]

Since 1930, as America became more technically advanced and more women entered the marketplace, breast feeding has declined. Formula companies make more money if mothers use sources other than their own. McDonald's advertises meat and potatoes, and many parents do not require children to eat green vegetables. Many parents simply have eliminated them from dinner because their children don't eat them. I know some of my readers who were taught nutrition sponsored by "agribusiness" are wondering where is the source of protein if not from meat. The same source as the cow, GREEN. All food has protein, including fruit, vegetables, nuts, legumes and grains.

My desire in this section is not to advocate vegetarianism, but to raise issues that may motivate thought about nutrition in another way. I do not wish to eliminate what is prepared, but to make sure the following is included; green vegetables, wheat products, salad, fruits, vitamins, and a larger intake of water. Nutrition is a major factor in child development which is greatly ignored. What mothers do in prenatal and postnatal stages affects self-esteem and discipline. What we feed our children, especially for breakfast, affects their ability and enthusiasm to learn. I am often disappointed when my children have their friends spend the night, and I observe their dietary preferences. They usually do not eat the ends of the bread, or green vegetables. I know it's not their fault; they were allowed to do this by their parents. Many adults have left the parenting profession and entered the "pleasing industry." Often, parents want to please children rather than do what is best for them. I believe a parent should "call them as they see them". The tragedy is that this generation of nutrition-deprived children will raise a future generation in similar fashion.

Role of Television

Studies also show that if the dinner hour includes television, conversation ceases. Television ranks as one of the major parental concerns. My experience has taught me that television, peer group, discipline, and single parenting are of utmost interest to parents. There are numerous books devoted solely to the subject of television. Three books I would strongly recommend are *Should Television Be the Primary Educator of Our Youth* by Niani Kilkenny, *The Four Arguments For the Elimination of Television* by Jerry Mander, and *The Disappearance of Childhood* by Neil Postman. I believe we have blamed the wrong source. As powerful as the TV media has become, they have, as yet, been unable to force us to turn it on! If television is a problem, it's because we have not *monitored* its use. Television actually is different from programming. The former is the equipment, and the latter is the content. A major problem is the content, and specifically, who is in control. The advancement of cable, video recorders, and those rare shows produced by people sensitive to developing positive images to Black children provide some possibilities. It would be erroneous for me to flatly condemn television and be a frequent guest on TV talk shows.

The four major problems are: TV dulls the senses, causes physical damages, promotes commercialism, and causes information loss[5]. The first problem is the dulling, and often deadening, of the senses. Television viewing does not require all of your intellect, it does not encourage thinking skills, and many people use it to put themselves to sleep. Programmers discount intelligence so much, they even insert laughter to cue the viewer on when it's time to laugh! I often hear children say, "I'm bored and there's nothing to do". What they really mean is that there is nothing to *watch*, and they don't know *how* to do anything. Boredom results when there is nothing on the inside. In African culture the word is "innerattainment" versus in Euro-American culture the word is "entertainment". In this society there is a separation between audience and performer, best illustrated by television, operas and hero/heroine worship. In African culture when the drummers play, the people dance; when the minister speaks the people respond. I often remember speaking to a large group of white educators where three women on separate occasions remarked to me, "You made me feel so good I felt like saying Amen". After the third time, it finally dawned on me: had this been a Black group they would have actually said "Amen".

Television viewing makes our children passive spectators. If you're watching television you're not reading, swimming, playing an instrument, sewing, drawing, skating, or participating in any meaningful activity. A bored person is created by being frequently entertained. They have not developed any other proficiencies except watching television — which requires none.

The second problem is physical damage to the brain and/or the eyes. Many op thalmologists believe television, which requires only straight-ahead staring, weakens the eye muscles that control the left-to-right or right-to-left motion required in reading. Jerry Mander in *The Four Arguments for the Elimination of Television* explains that,

> television's light is projected into our eyes from behind the screen by cathode-ray guns which are literally aimed at us. These guns are powered by 25,000 volts in color television, and about 15,000 volts in the black-and-white sets. Artificial light from any source, whether incandescent or fluorescent, leaves out many segments of the spectral range contained in natural light, and it delivers an entire different mix of spectral ingredients. The effect on the body, called malillumination, causes disorders ranging from lack of vitality to lowered resistance to disease and hyperactivity. The Emoy report shows brain waves slow down the longer television is viewed.[6]

The third problem is commercialism. Our children see 50,000 commercials a year. They see it, they want it; they want their world to look like the world on television. Television is the media that sells products not values. How do you advertise honesty, integrity, morality, and commitment? Television is a visual media that works best with visual images and products. It does a better job highlighting the features of a Datsun 280Z and designer jeans than the values of sacrifices, denials, and causes. The sponsor only provides the show as a lead into their product. Do you think GM, Ford, Chrysler, Sears, United and Budweiser would pay upwards of $300,000 for a thirty-second commercial in the hope that you will enjoy the superbowl game? The advent of mass production created mass media and mass consumption. What advertisements must do is give the illusion to the consumer that their product is a need. When women feel they need a new pair of shoes, with ten pairs in the closet; and when men say they need a Cadillac instead of a less expensive car, it proves that sponsors have done their job quite well.

Saturday morning programming for children is actually criminal, and has provoked many adversary groups to monitor and protest both the programming and the commercials that are filled with sugary foods and toys. Children are virtual prey to the sophisticated Fifth Avenue marketers. The following scenario best describes the effects of television:

> "I am home from school, Mommy," Little Johnny yells as he
> runs to his room to watch HIS TV.
> But his mother doesn't hear Little Johnny yell because
> she is watching a soap on HER TV.
> Little Johnny throws his books on his unmade bed. His
> spelling test falls on the floor.
> Little Johnny sits and wonders how he spelled those
> two words wrong.
> He heard them spelled a thousand times in the TV
> song.
> He thought he knew those words so well and didn't
> have to guess.
> He was absolutely certain that "cheese" is spelled
> K-R-A-F-T.
> and 'relief" is spelled R-O-L-A-I-D-S!"[7]

The last problem is information loss. The average Black household watches television eight hours daily. The Black family is dependent on a media they do not control for their images and interpretation of the world. The images and frame of reference provided by the media are not designed to develop positive self-images and discipline in Black children. The lack of stable families, responsible Black men, and serious discussion presented on TV is by intent not by accident. The foreign policy emphasis on Israel and not the removal of minority rule in South Africa should motivate Black families to utilize alternative sources of information.

The increasing influence of television has reduced the role of other forms of media in the dissemination of information. This trend is reflected with the death of the afternoon newspaper. If you did a survey of your neighborhood on their source of news, television would be the overwhelming winner. News from print sources or direct via meetings, workshops, conferences and conversations are underutilized. People make decisions based on information, therefore, to control information is to determine people's decisions. Many people feel issues and people only become legitimate when they're on television. Gil Scott Heron may be correct when he said, "The Revolution will not be televised," but if you want the masses to be there or *believe* it's taking place, it may have to be aired.

At the outset, I indicated a major problem was the lack of parental monitoring of television. Listed below are several strategies to use when the television is on. First, you should check off in the TV Guide the shows you want your child to watch. They should watch only what you want them to watch if a level of trust exists between you and your children. Secondly, a recommended maximum limit of two hours per day should be established. The American average is seven, and Black households watch eight hours per day. I do not believe a limit of two hours will make our children deprived. Next, as much as possible, watch shows with your children. Our children need to be taught critical thinking skills versus becoming passive viewers. The game of "needs and wants" can be played with the commercials. During the commercial, the children can determine whether it is advertising one or the other. This same game can be played at the grocery and department store.

Lastly, I recommend playing the game I call "1910." This game requires nothing but your imagination. Once a week, your family should imagine it is the year 1910, when there was no television. After your children recover from the shock of no television, start playing concentration (a game with a deck of cards turned over), chess, checkers, Password, Scrabble, Boggle, Uno, and other thinking games. Take your children on field trips — with special emphasis on nature — and the library. My inclination, with any subject, is to take the "pro" versus "anti" position. Telling your children not to watch television is the negative; taking your child to music lessons, swim class, library, nature hikes, etc. is the positive, but these activities require parental support. The home program I advocate must go beyond "go outside and play or watch television", it starts wtih imagining you're living in 1910.

Single Parenting

An issue affecting many families is single parenting. This parental state has reached epidemic proportion. The problem is a national problem with 67 million people single. Forty percent of all families are headed by a woman, and only 13 percent of all families fitting the traditional mode of two parents with the mother at home. For the Black community, it translates into 62 percent of all its children living in a single run household.[8] Of course, the problem is not single parenting, because it takes two to make a baby. The concern is, what happened to the men? The definition of manhood adhered to by most people is being the breadwinner. An effective strategy to destroy Black men is to deny them the opportunity to work, and to create welfare legislation that encourages and mandates their removal from the household. Black women are left with two options; either ignore the impact that institutional racism and white male supremacy has on her man, with no compassion; or provide understanding, encouragement, and supplemental income. The first option further alienates the Black family, and the second, while preferred, is not totally acceptable to Black men who continue to look to white society for approval rather than to their family. It takes **a secure, well informed man and woman to cope with male unemployment and remain harmonious.** The book *Countering the Conspiracy to Destroy Black Boys* is an attempt to develop this sensitive awareness, and to intervene before the problem is manifested. This part of the book will attempt to understand the issue of single parents.

The family structure has changed with the economy. When the economy was agriculturally based and employment was higher, the family structure was based on the extended family concept. This economy encouraged large numbers of children and relatives. The economy that followed was based on factory production. This system was geared toward urbanization and required less labor, and the family structure responded with the nuclear family. Children were less desired in this economy, creating the need for mass public education from primary grades through high school. The present economy of computerization encourages greater mobility than previous economies which were tied to land and factory. But the new economy, based on information, encourages movement of people as quickly as you move information. This economy has even less need for children and workers. Marriages have historically provided economic security to women, but this new economy, where women work just as much if not more than men, makes each part economically independent. This contributes to the large incidence of divorce in our society, compounded in the Black community because of high male unemployment.

The five major problems of single parenting are: the lack of time, lack of money, loneliness, children's acceptance of the situation, and the missing role model — which 90 percent of the time will be male. Simple mathematics illustrate that, with one parent versus two, there will be less time given to the children. A mother wraps a blanket around the coat of her almost three-year-old daughter and treks out of the house a full sixty minutes before the sun will appear, headed for the day care center which now opens at 6:00 a.m. She arrives at 6:30 and proceeds downtown by bus to start work at 7:30, completes a demanding work day, picks her daughter up at 5:15, and arrives home at 5:45 for dinner, dishes, housework, family time, bath, and, hopefully, personal time.

The story of the mother who began and ended her day in the dark reflects how tight and precious time is for the single parent. Time is not a problem exclusively confined to single parents; people of both sexes and different races stress the need for time management. Time, like any other resource, needs to be managed wisely, and some people do a better job than others. But the first step is to plan how your time is to be spent, and compare your projection to the actual events for modification. Time-saving tips include; cooking the night before, a clean-as-you cook approach to dinner to avoid stacks of dirty dishes, limited television viewing, and developing children's self reliance. But more importantly, there is a difference between quality and quantity time with your children. Watching television or simply being under the same roof is not spending time with your children, but at your children. I advocate spending time with your children where you allocate quality time and ask them what they want to do with you. They may just want to look and touch you. Or they may want to talk with you or play their special game. But whatever they want within reason, try to comply because, to them, when serious issues affect their lives, they will know they have a parent who is a friend who will listen, which has become rare among parents.

Financial problems, while not confined to single parents, affect them more often because they have the responsibility of raising what two people decided to produce. Fortunately, some single parents receive support from the other parent, or have an adequate income-earning position. Others less fortunate should, first, improve their marketable skills by returning to school; second, manage their money by developing a budget based on needs rather than wants; and frequently compare their projection to the actual budget for adjustment.

Many single parents express loneliness in two areas; seeking opposite-sex companionship, and having another adult near to share the joys and pains of parenting. Oftentimes, single parents feel guilty when they possess these feelings, and they ignore their own needs and immerse themselves exclusively into their children, which could lead to greater frustration and susceptibility to child abuse. Single parents need to acknowledge their true feelings, find a vehicle for expression, and seek the assistance of the extended family for support. Some single parents devote all of their time to the children and lose a part of themselves. Others do the exact opposite, to the neglect of the children. Single parents should use discretion and be selective on who, when, and where they expose their "friends" to their children. Being a single *parent* is different from single paren*ting*. The former allows the possibility for neighbors and relatives to assume some responsibility, while the latter places it all on one person.

Children's acceptance of the lost parent concerns itself not only with the reality of living with one parent, but also accepting the fact that their parent may begin to date other people. Parents must be very open and honest with their children if they expect them to become sensitive. Many children can't imagine their parents ever being children or having needs and feelings that sometimes made them laugh and cry. Children miss the very enriching experience of being considerate and sensitive if their parent attempts to be a super person. Children should want their parents to be happy, and they should be raised to understand that life's objectives transcend their own desires.

The missing role model for children—either the male or female, but more often times the male—needs to be corrected not only for sons but also for daughters. It's fairly obvious that sons need a positive male image, but if daughters do not see and understand the role men should play in family life they will have little appreciation and knowledge of how to interact in the future. We must resist America's racist attack to destroy Black men, and the "scholarly condemnation" that claims Black women run Black men away. Nor can we accept their definition of the family as being nuclear, which prevents our extended male models—grandfather, uncle, brother-in-law, nephew, cousin, and neighbor—from contributing a positive image. In addition, good parents understand the tremendous impact that the peer group has on children by programming them into extracurricular activities with peers who reinforce the goals and values of the parent—martial arts, dancing, athletics, band, etc.

The issue of single parenting is complex and rapidly increasing. To successfully handle this unnatural situation requires information about the contributing societal circumstances and the five major problems, soul searching, and acceptance. I know a lot of single parents who are doing a much better job than their two-parent counterparts. Often, two parents who remain married communicate poorly and do not share responsibilities; many women in this situation describe a feeling of single parenting while still married. Often these parents give a sigh of relief when they are "officially" single because the tension, bitterness, and animosity are gone, and peace has been restored. The most important factor in developing positive images and discipline is not numbers, but genuine care and concern. The combination of quality time, greater utilization of the extended family, and guided peer group activities can make single parenting successful.

*　*　*　*　*

The objective of this chapter was to better understand how parents can develop positive self-images and discipline in Black children. The achievement of this goal requires an acknowledgement that the parent is the first and primary educator. It also requires a home program which will provide children with experiences and opportunities to develop their God-given talents. Consistency, praise, and positive parental role models give children a very good start in developing a secure self-esteem. The last and concluding chapter provides strategies that teachers, parents and education researchers can implement to achieve the title of this book.

Questions/Exercises/Projects.

1) What can parents do to become the primary educator?

2) What can be done to improve the relationship between the school and home?

3) Describe your home program when you play 1910.

Chapter 6
From Theory to Practice: Strategies for Success

This final chapter provides strategies that may develop positive self-images and discipline in Black children. This entire book comes out of my concern for hearing words without movement, talk without action. It has been said many times that a people who do not learn their history are destined to repeat it. This statement implies that once you know your history, you will not make the same mistake again. The statement appears perfectly logical. It leads us to believe that if we make our history available, and bring the truth to our people they will respond; and that through our knowledge and self determination, we will not make the same mistakes again.

Theory Inadequacies

Each year there are local, national, and international conferences about improving the conditions of African-Americans. There are people in our midst who are professional conference-goers. One of the larger airlines publishes a directory that lists conferences for nearly every week of the year. The conferences use such fancy slogans from "Where Do We Go From Here" to "The State of the Race". They become star-studded with the "baddest" educators, historians, musicians, poets, feminists, Marxists, nationalists, etc. The typical conference is divided up into workshops, keynote speeches, and parties. Somewhere along the line you are to assume that the slogans, question or themes will not only be addressed, but answered and followed up with structural policies.

The movement from theory to practice has not been achieved. The logical conclusion then is that the issue required more time than was allocated, and that it will be addressed again at a follow-up conference. Another observation would be that with the large number of conferences and the large number of professional conference-goers, their accumulated experience would allow them to solve these questions at the following week's conference. This again has not been the case. Is it because we have not read our history? Is it because we have not analyzed the issues correctly? Is it because we really don't want to solve the issues? Solving the issues would remove the need for conferences and theoreticians. Herbert Gans in an analysis concerning poverty states, "Without poverty, a large section of people would be unemployed. If there were no poverty there would be no need for social workers."[1]

The Black community has within it a group of theoretical intellectuals that talks to itself. Each program attracts the same people. Each program allows the same people to talk to each other. This environment provides security for all of the members, because very few new faces enter the circle. In this way, change is not required. Everyone is able to theorize about whatever they want, because the people who need the information, the people who would implement this information are not included. Very little attention is given to why such groups continue to be made up of the same faces. The rationale is often given that "the masses are not ready." Further discussion brings such statements as, "You always have one to ten percent who do most of the work". This provides a great degree of security for the members because they feel they are assuming the burden of the race by being in such an elite group. Frequently, at these gathering someone will say, "I agree with what has been said but how do we involve the masses." Because that person is viewed as a novice in this kind of group, her/his ideas are considered inconsistent with the goals and objectives of the larger group. The intellectual community will sometimes respond very honestly and sophistictedly and say, "We agree that this information needs to go to the masses, but we don't have those kinds of resources" or, "That is not our objectives," or, "That is not our interest." Imagine the leadership of the community not having an objective to organize the community. The immediate response should be, "What is our objective?"

How sweet the words of Mari Evans, "Speak the truth to the people." Our people have been lied to and given false promises. Black people are cautious. They will listen to what you say, but will judge by what they see. The major question constantly asked is "Now that we know the problem, what do we do about it?" How do we develop positive self-images and discipline in Black children? The answer to this question cannot be answered with words. To answer this question requries action. Developing an anti-position on various issues requires analysis; providing alternatives demands work. Similarly, turning on television does not provide a home program filled with library, swimming, skating, music lessons, and family games.

Deterrents to "Practice"

I belive the reason we have not moved from theory to practice is because of money, work, fear, and faith. Many of us could not quit our jobs tomorrow. The upcoming check has already been committed to Visa, car note, and mortgage. We want to help Black children, but choose to compromise for financial expediency. Many of us secured our position through the agitation and hard work of the 1960's but have not repaid the debt. This debt cannot be resolved with an annual contribution to your favorite charity, but only with a sincere committment of time and money.

The second deterrent is lack of work. To provide your child with a home program, or to volunteer in a community project providing children with tangible skills would require work. The Black community suffers because we spend and work outside of it. Most of us spend eight hours working, two hours for round trip transportation, three hours for breakfast, lunch, and dinner; followed by eight hours of sleeping; totalling twenty-one hours, resulting in three hours remaining to be divided between, television, telephone, music, and reading. To improve our volunteer efforts requires both dedication and time management skills.

Third, is the issue of fear, the feeling that too much expression of self-determination will bring about physical repercussions. The more success Black organizations achieve in negotiating their "fair share" the greater the risk that it may eventually lead to physical reprisal. Malcolm X often said, "Africans fight for land while Negroes march over lunch counters." I sincerely believe that we do not need martyrs, people who will die for the struggle. Martin Luther King and Malcolm X both believed if you haven't found something to live for, you are already dead.

Last, is the lack of faith. Deep in our hearts, many of us do not believe that Black people can think and take care of ourselves. The current dilemma is that many parents have not taken the responsibility to be the primary educator, and many teachers do not believe Black children can learn. The burning desire to develop Black children has eroded from the home and one-room school shack. The dilemma in white citadels of political power is not the stated question of "Why can't Johnny learn?" but a more diabolical concept of "Should Johnny learn?"

The Negro question is, what are they going to do for us? The African question is, what are we going to do for ouselves? I provide three answers to the African question: advocate, supplement, and build our own independent institutions. Our history has not been all bleak. We have some success stories that need to be told.

Advocate and Inform

This category includes institutions and individuals who recognize that the largest number of African-Americans presently attend public schools because the accessibility of private schools is not an option available to the masses of children. This group chooses to advocate for them and provide information that maybe useful. Institutions that consistently have advocated for our children are the National Association of Black Psychologists, the Association of Black Social Workers, and the Association of Black School Educators. This book is an endorsement of their efforts and an encouragement for your participation.

I want to isolate the excellent work of National Black Child Development Institute (NBCDI). It was founded in 1970 as a nonprofit membership organization dedicated to improving the quality of life for Black children and their families, through public policy advocacy. Their focus falls within the areas of child care, child welfare, and education. NBCDI consists of over thirty local affiliates, designed to bring Black professionals together for internal development and external advocacy.

A coalition of NBCDI, Children Defense Fund, and numerous other advocacy groups, work closely with programs such as Headstart and Chapter I to fight the onslaught of Federal budget cuts. The efforts of advocacy are best expressed by studies reporting that without Headstart there are millions of children who would not have received nutritious meals, vaccinations, dental and medical care or preschool services. The Perry Preschool Project, a longitudinal study of low income children, confirms the sustained effects of educational gains made during this period. They have calculated that only medical schools have a higher return on the dollar invested. Headstart is cost effective.

Chapter I consistently reports the sustained effects of educating children. Chapter I has a 34 percent Black component, while only 19 percent of the total public school population is Black. The benefits gained by Black children who participate in Chapter I are indicated in their improved test scores and their achievement gains maintained over the summer when their non-Chapter I peers demonstrated achievement losses. Chapter I students also benefit from a higher level of instructional resources than their non-participating peers, and by active parent involvement. [1]

The other component of this category is information, the research and dissemination of ideas which may enhance the development of our children. The dissemination of ideas takes the form of staff in-service training, parent workshops, and children's assembly programs. I have provided workshops for teachers, parents, and students since 1975. I am strongly convinced that effective schools avoid stagnation with a constant flow of information to all parties.

Researching ideas is vital to insure sound theoretical direction. Coleman and Lensen reported that low achievement by poor children derived principally from inherent disabilities characterizing the poor. Weber was an early contributor to the refutation of the above. In his study of four instructionally-effective inner-city schools, reading proficiency was clearly successful for poor children when compared to national achievement scores. Weber's contention is that socioeconomic factors were not decisive in child development but that these four schools had an environment conducive for learning. Additional studies by Madden, Edmonds, and Brookover confirm and support Weber's contention that socioeconomic factors are not as significant in student performance as teacher expectations. [2]

Studies, Projects and Practices

A growing body of research indicates that, for like populations of students, some schools are more instructionally effective than others. While the identified factors among the studies vary in number, all seem to contain these seven basic principles.

1. A Sense of Mission
Effective schools make a conscious decision to become effective schools and that is their mission. A decision and commitment is made to assure minimum mastery of basic school skills for all pupils. Acquisition of basic school skills takes precedence over all other school activities and, when necessary, school energy and resources are diverted from other activities to achieve that end.

2. Leadership
Effective schools have principals who are, in fact, the instructional leaders of the staff. They are creative, bold, supportive and dedicated to the mission of the school. They are active and involved with all parts of their educational community.

3. High Expectations for All Students and Staff

Effective schools expect teachers to teach and pupils to learn. Standards are high but realistic. No student is allowed to attain less than minimum mastery of the basic skills of the assigned level. Teachers believe that they have the ability to provide the required instructional program and that all students can master basic skills.

4. Frequent Monitoring of Student Progress

Effective schools have teachers and principals who are constantly aware of pupil progress in relationship to the instructional objectives. Frequent monitoring of pupil progress may be as traditional as classroom testing on the day's lesson or as advanced as criterion-referenced, system-wide, standardizes testing measures.

5. A Positive Learning Climate

Effective schools have an atmosphere that is orderly without being rigid, quiet without being oppressive, and generally conducive to the instructional mission. The climate is warm and responsive, emphasizes cognitive development, is innovating, and provides a student support system.

6. Sufficient Opportunity for Learning

Effective schools emphasize more time on task. The more time spent in instruction, the greater the learning that takes place. Implications exist for improved use of time, individualized instruction and curriculum content.

7. Parent/Community Involvement

Effective schools have broad support, parents influence their children in a number of ways through their expectations for the children through their own involvement, and through direct instructions.[3]

Brookover in *Creative Effective Schools* provides practical illustrations of the above theoretical design.

The George Washington Carver School is composed predominantly of black, working class children who are achieving well above the state average. On a recent visit, the Carver staff was asked. "How do you account for your success?" Mrs. Johns, an experienced teacher, answered for the staff, "We are all in this together. We have a job to do. If Johnny doesn't learn to read today, we will see to it that he learns to read tomorrow."

In contrast a Black fifth grade teacher, separated from her husband, moved herself and her three children from Louisiana to Illinois. Her job in a black inner city school had gone well. She had called or visited every parent of her students. Eighty percent of the parents responded that she was the first teacher to communicate positively with them. After a time she began hearing subtle hints about being a "do-gooder" and an "apple polisher" from her fellow teachers. When these hints became less subtle, she was forced to start having lunch by herself in her room. It was not long before she was told that "the way it is here is not to make waves. Keep the kids quiet with busywork, and read your paper while they copy out of the encyclopedia." She continued her remedial reading work and teaching with high expectations. The first illustration describes an effective learning climate. It clearly assumes that all students can learn. The entire staff has accepted the responsibility to teach all children. Results began to show, even though most of her students were far below grade level. Remarks about a woman alone with three children being in a precarious situation really shook her up, but she persevered with her teaching efforts. Finally, she was told outright to conform or to expect physical consequences to herself, her family, car, or home. She returned to Louisiana. The learning climate of the school remains unchanged and the achievement level remains extremely low.[4]

The second case starkly portrays the negative sanctions and the power of the social group to set standards and norms for the school. Often, if these norms are unprofessional, a good teacher becomes a social isolate or finally conforms to the negative standards.

Some teachers may defend this behavior as merely "blowing off steam" or expressing frustration, with no harm intended. My answer to that is, intended or not, this type of atmosphere leads to lower expectations and evaluations of student ability. Additionally, the very fact that there is a need to "blow off steam" in one school while another school does not evidence the same frustration is itself a reflection of the differing levels of the school learning climate. Brookover suggests the formation of "climate watchers", a self-help group of teachers who will assess the environment, declare objectives, provide support and sensitivity sessions, and monitors negative conversations frequently heard in teacher lounges and in the corridors.

Fortunately, we hear more and more about the need for increased teacher expectations. This challenge sounds simple: high expectations produce high achievers, low expectations produce low achievers. Listed below are frequent obstacles to high expectations with which lowered academic expectations are associated:

1. Sex. Lower expectations for elementary boys and older girls. This is a function of belief about boys slower maturation and sex role discrimination for older girls.
2. Socioeconomic factors lower expectations for children depending on parental education, types of jobs held, place or residence, etc.
3. Race. Lower expectations for African-Americans
4. Test scores, permanent records. Belief in "fixed ability" precludes possibility of improvement and higher expectations;
5. Type of school, rural, inner city, or suburban. The first two are associated with lower expectations;
6. Appearance. Lower expectations associated with clothes or grooming that are out of style, cheaper material, etc.
7. Oral language patterns. Negative cues from any non-standard English result in lower expectations;
8. Student behavior. Lower academic expectations for students with poor behavior;

To provide children with a home program or community project which develops tangible

---

9. Tracking or grouping. Labeling effects and a tendency to accentuate differences between students result in lower expectations.[5]

The major obstacles to high expectations are sex, race, economics, test scores, residency, appearance, language, behavior, and tracking. Teachers should reflect on the above and probe themselves to see if these factors affect their perceptions.

A study of schooling was conducted by John Goodlad. This study, considered the largest ever undertaken, covered eight years and included twenty trainers. It looked at thirteen communities in seven sections of the country, producing a sample of 38 schools differing in several significant characteristics. The data was drawn from 8,624 parents, 1,350 teachers, 17,163 students, and over 1,000 classrooms.[6]

There were numerous recommendations derived from the study, but there are two I wish to accentuate. They include time on task,

requires the participation of adults who are sensitve and caring as well as knowledgeable.

and grouping or tracking. Society often refers to public schools as if they are all monolithic. I frequently remind people that Chicago public schools provide a range of institutions, some called "magnet" schools with a four-year waiting list highlighting certain curriculum areas, and "general" schools. One in particular started and ended a school year with 1,500 students, but 800 students moved in and out through the transient semester. John Goodlad reports a school range of instructional time from as low as eighteen and one-half hours to a high of twenty-seven and one half hours per week.[7] Studies done by Bloom in *Learning for Mastery* show that, on the average, the difference between mastery and non-mastery for a student needing corrective instruction is about an hour of extra instruction every two weeks; this is the equivalent of six minutes per school day.[8]

Time on task is crucial for achievement; yet, time management varies greatly from school to school and even classroom to classroom. A typical school day is from 9:00 to 3:00, or six hours. Subtracting the hour for lunch plus or minus recess will leave, on the average for most schools, five hours per day or twenty-five hours per week. If one classroom or school provides just one-half hour less instruction per day, multiplied by five days and forty weeks, it creates a deficiency of 100 hours per year. If six minutes per day as previously cited is significant, 100 hours become catastrophic for academic achievement. Goodlad also notes "school with less instructional time decrease time allocated to social studies, science, foreign language, fine arts etc."[9] Administrators and teachers should take a critical look at projected versus actual time for instruction, discipline and absenteeism, and their affect on time allocation.

A major component of the "effective schools project" is the education of *all* students, not just selected students. Tracking or homogenous grouping continues in spite of research confirming its perpetuation of the self-fulfilling prophecy. Goodlad comments,

> High track classes spent a larger proportion of class time on instruction, and their teachers expected students to spend more time learning at home than was the case in the low tracks. Other research shows that the level of the groups in which a child participated most regular in the primary grades is highly predictive of track placement later: high, middle or low. Studies have shown there to be lower self-esteem, more school misconduct, higher drop out rates, and higher delinquency among students in lower tracks. Track placement affects whether or not students plan to go to college and the probability of their acceptance, over and beyond the effects of aptitude and grades. Minority students and those from the lowest socioeconomic groups have been found in disproportionate numbers in classes at the lowest track levels, and children from upper socioeconomic levels have been found consistently over-represented in higher tracks. Tracking prevails because it is perceived to be a logical and expedient way to take account of wide differences in students' academic attainments. In effect, however, it seems as an organizational device for hiding awareness of the problem rather than an educative means for correcting it. The decision to track is essentially one of giving up on the problem and the evidence of different expectations should be proof enough.[10]

The issue of tracking is very complex but, while banned from many school districts, the practice unofficially continues. Learning ability varies from student to student, and heterogenous grouping can cause boredom for advanced learners and frustration for others. My three suggestions are: consistent teacher expectations for all students regardless of tracking, mutual student cooperation, and enrichment programs for students in need. The major problem with tracking is that quite often students in lower tracks remain because of low teacher expectations. The competitive nature among students perpetuates the problem and prevents the collective support between peers.

Supplemental Programs

The second strategy, after advocating and disseminating information, is supplemental programs. These projects take the form of tutoring, dance, drama, history, peer group development, etc. Many programs provide a combination of the above, while some concentrate in one area. This approach is very similar to the Jewish community that supplements their children's public education with "culture" classes. Black groups nationwide can be found operating on evening and weekends. There are numerous groups, often overlooked, providing a fine service in the aforementioned areas.

The satisfaction that accrues from this type of involvement is largely due to direct contact. Oftentimes, our ideologies take us away from the people that we identify as needing to be served, whereas a volunteer in a supplemental program is able to transmit his/her ideology directly to the child. This approach can start as easily as rounding up the children on your block, and providing constructive activities.

Supplemental and enrichment programs can be viewed as permanent in structure, or a stepping stone to full-time instruction. Numerous independent schools and other institutions started as weekday/weekend activities. The major objective here is not to compare any form of involvement, advocacy/research, supplemental, or full time institutions, but to encourage all those concerned about African-American children to become involved.

The W.E.B. DuBois Learning Center located in Kansas City, Missouri is a recommended model of this category. This group of dedicated men and women are clear on their objectives, and function cohesively to produce a quality program. The purpose of the center is to offer enrichment and remedial tutorial services in academic skills to children in the Kansas City area. Founded in 1974, the center has concentrated on reading and mathemathics. The reading program is essentially remedial and caters to grade levels one through eight. It consists of three basic groups: grade levels one through three, four and five, and six through eight. The mathematics program which has five basic levels was the first and thus far the most successful program. The range is from pre-school through college-level courses. Classes are conducted three times a week, twice on weekday evenings, and Saturday morning. In addressing the questions of facilities and purpose, I quote from their manual:

> When I look at churches, bars, etc. in our community "I" see more than churches, bars, etc. "I" see buildings that our community controls, that could be used to educate our children. As the word of the learning center spreads and we continue to grow, we hope to be a model for other churches, community centers, etc. who are interested in working with young people. Cabral teaches us: "Always bear in mind that the people are not fighting for ideas, for things in anyone's head (theory and ideology). They are fighting to win material benefits (goods and/or services), to live better in peace, to see their lives go forward, to guarantee the future of their children. The program has grown to 250 children, and parents continue to bring their children, not because of our philosophy, but, because they see progress in their children.[11]

I have had the fortunate experience of working with the above group and the major lesson I learned was that their success is attributed to their consistency. Many Black programs commence and fold almost simultaneously, because the Black community becomes hesitant about lending support at the outset. This problem is exacerbated by the instability of governmental funding. The joke in Kansas City is, "Does the W.E.B. DuBois tutoring program still exist?" The answer for the past ten years has been unequivocally yes!

While there are numerous other programs teaching Black children dance, drama, Black History etc., that this book will be unable to mention, I do want to spotlight one more. This program operating in several cities is the Simba Wachanga Program (Swahili for young lions). The Simba program is an attempt to develop Black boys into men. The objectives of the program are to provide skill development, Black History, recreation, adult male role models, and the rites of passage into manhood, taking into consideration both African tradition and twenty-first century reality. Listed below is an outline on how to start a Simba program.

1. Organize a group of Black men willing to participate in the program.

2. Develop study sessions with the above group discussing Black history and male development. Recommended titles are *Countering The Conspiracy To Destroy Black Boys, Black Masculinity, Home is a Dirty Street, Black Men, Hazards of Being a Male, Autobiography of Malcolm X, Tally's Corner, Miseducation of the Negro, Destruction of Black Civilization, There is a River,* and *The Choice.*

3. Decide on a facility, and the frequency and length of the meeting with the young brothers. (Age is discretionary).

4. Recommended schedule would be weekly, with one week each allocated to a field trip, Black History, skill development, and "rites of passage" (male socialization).

5. Field trips should include a prison, drug abuse center, teenage pregnancy center, public hospital emergency room on a Saturday evening, best suburban high-school, stock market, camping, and computer oriented businesses.[12]

Independent Institutions

The last category of involvement is the building of independent, Black institutions. This movement is in direct opposition to *Brown* vs *Topeka* in 1954, declaring "we can take care of ourselves". Black colleges still produce 40 percent of all Black graduates, yet only have 20 percent of the students. In contrast, 80 percent of all Black students go to white universities yet these institutions produce only 60 percent of the graduates.[13]. The Black college historically has been committed to the development of its students, versus white colleges interested more in federal dollars for Black enrollment. Unfortunately, Black colleges are suffering because of desegration policies that question the need for Black colleges. The future of Black colleges is dependent on how much Black people value them.

Other success stories in the area of independent Black institutions are Westside Prep operated in Chicago by Marva Collins, and Providence St. Mel, also in Chicago, directed by Paul Adams. Both schools are located on the West side of the city in a low-income area. They are both privately operated with parents scuffling to pay tuition that never meets the entire budget. Pride in the school had brought success to their fundraising efforts. Marva Collins and Paul Adams both believe in the commercial, "We do it the old fashion way: We earn it." Westside Prep students are reading one to three years above grade level, and Providence St. Mel has upward of 95 percent of its graduating class destined for college.

Another success story is The Council of Independent Black Institutions (CIBI), forty independent pre and elementary schools nationwide. Black educators, parents, and community people met and strategized viable methods of sustaining community-controlled schools. One of these meetings occurred in East Palo Alto, California in August 1970, cosponsored by the California Association for Afro-American Education and Nairobi College. It was April 21, 1972, in

New York, that the Council of Independent Black Institutions was officially formed with fourteen charter members. The subsequent years have produced additional members, the establishment of an annual national teachers training institute, and an annual science fair as a vehicle for Black excellence. Their ideology includes this four-point platform:

1) To develop their bodies through proper diet and daily exercise.
2) To develop their minds by acquiring knowledge and skills useful in the Black liberation struggle.
3) To develop their consciousness by attaining self-awareness (identity) and self-control (discipline).
4) To develop their souls by practicing the social relationships based on the Nguzo Saba (seven principles in the Black Value System), i.e. Umoja (unity), Kujichagulia (self-determination), Ujima (collective work and responsibility), Ujamaa (cooperative economics), Nia (purpose), Kuumba (creativity), and Imani (faith)[14]

The federal government is also pleased with their success, but for a different motive; the legislation concerning tuition tax credit. The disproportionate percentage of Black children attending public schools has reduced the national commitment to public education. The Black community must intervene and not allow Black public educators to be manipulated against each other.

I opened this book with a dedication to children. I consider myself an advocate for them. I believe they have a message to tell, if only we will listen. I encourage adults to attempt to see the world through the eyes of children. I wonder how many adults in this new era could do as well as our children. From my experience working with children, I would like to offer two other strategies: The first is to allow them to frequently teach each other. The peer group continues to gain influence but, if properly coordinated, could provide wholesome development. Research has found that peer relationships strongly influence student feelings about the importance of academic performance, and about the appropriateness of such behavior as studying, cheating, skipping school, and going to college. Research on team learning provides us with evidence that this technique is valuable because it improves the overall climate.[15]. Children should become each other's tutors. Success should be based on a class grade versus individual achievement. Debates, bees, Black History contests, etc., should be administered through team rather than individual competition.

My second suggestion is to take another look at what we expect children to do between the ages of four and eighteen. I believe that many adults do not know what to do with youth. In previous economies, we put them to work at an early age, but with this present economy, children are not needed until... when? We have instilled in them the belief that education is a result rather than a process. Children still believe at the magical age of sixteen, eighteen or twenty-one, that "real life" begins. This anticipation has been further stimulated by children being exposed to the same information as adults via mass media. We now have a generation of children who know what we know but have been placed in an indefinite holding pattern until we know what to do with them. Robert Meeker notes:

> There used to be an obvious correspondence between the skills we learned in school and their application in the work world. There's almost none now. Schools do not foster an attitude of responsibility that is required at work. I have a vision of a school that would prepare students better for the world of work. Why not make school units of production in society. Miniature business with employees and employers made of students would be an integral part of the curriculum.[16]

Most people tell Meeker that he's crazy, but think about it. People also thought Goodlad was off the course when he questioned the reverence of first through twelfth grade. Goodlad suggests starting children at age four (most children are in school at this age anyway). The concept would be three stages; four through seven, eight through eleven, and twelve through fifteen. Since those twelve years embrace what are now grades one through twelve, and also include kindergarten and the upper year of nursery school, we are considering accomplishing in twelve years what now, for many children, spreads over fourteen.[17] What is magical about pre-school through twelfth grade? Could we do it in shorter time? Would the alteration reduce the dropout rate, apathy and vandalism? Will the change allow youth time, upon completion, to creatively make decisions about the future while the interest still exists?

In conclusion: How do we develop positive self-images and discipline in Black children? Following are some strategies:

1. We must recognize that the majority of Black children have not been educated, and that this is not the priority of the one percent ruling class in America, and it is perpetuated by Black apathy.
2. The development of an African frame of reference, which would be the criteria for image selection.
3. The encouragement of thinking skills and relational applications to maintain children's curiosity and enthusiasm to learn.

4. The development of self-discipline motivated by a consistent, complementary, and assertive adult role model.
5. The first and primary educator of Black children is the parent, and he or she must establish a home program which creates experiences and opportunities to develop their child's God-given talents.
6. We must advocate the best services available for our children, establish high expectations, create supplemental programs, and build independent Black educational institutions.

*   *   *   *   *

The development of positive self-images and discipline in Black children is the primary responsibility of the parent. Teachers should provide supplemental nurturance and high expectations. If the parent does not fulfill his or her primary responsibility, every available institution must take heed to develop positive self-images and discipline in Black children.

References

CHAPTER 1

1) Green, Laura and Washington, Betty. "Grim Reality Casts Shadow Over Dreams," *Chicago Sun Times*, Feb. 14, 1983, pp. 27, 36.
2) *Washington Post*, April 17, 1978, p. 6.
3) U.S. Dept. of Labor, Bureau of Labor Statistic press release pp. 79-90.
4) Arnez, Nancy. "Implementation of Desegration as a Discriminating Process." *Journal of Negro Foundation*, 1978, pp. 28-45.
5) Wilhelm, Sidney. *Who Needs the Negro.* N.Y.: Schenkman Publishers, 1970, pp. IIX-XIV, pp. 332-334.
6) Curwood, Steve. "Minorities Face Grim Employment Future," *Chicago Sun Times*, Nov. 2, 1983, p. 74.
7) Nyerere, Julius. *Ujamaa: Essays on Socialism*, Dar es Salaam: Oxford 1968, pp. 44-75.
8) Hoyles, Martin, Ed. *Changing Childhood.* London: Writers and Readers Publishing Cooperative, 1979, pp. 3, 5, 7.
9) Postman, Neil, *The Disappearance of Childhood.* N.Y.: Delacorte Press, 1982, pp. 10, 13, 14, 18.
10) Atkinson, Pansye and Hord, Fred. "Save The Children", Office of Minority Affairs, Frostbury: 1983, pp. 3-4.
11) The USA: Who Owns It? *Black Liberation Month News*, People College Press, February 1984, p. 6
12) Hale, Janice. *Black Children.* Provo: Brigham Young University Press: 1982, p.3.
    Hale, Janice. "De-Mythicizing the Educating of Black Children," *First World*, May 1977, p. 30.
13) Woodson, Carter. *Miseducation of the Negro.* Washington D.C.: Associated Publishers, 1933, pp. XXXI, XXXIII, 5, 38.
14) National Black Studies Conference. Education Workshop, Professor Epps, March 1982.
15) Excerpts from "The Challenge of Blackness" delivered by Lerone Bennett at the Institute of the Black World in Atlanta, Georgia, 1972.
16) Hale, p. 30.
17) Williams, Robert. "Black Pride, Academic Relevance and Individual Achievement." St. Louis: Robert Williams and Associates, pp. 2-3.

CHAPTER 2

1) Berg, Paul. "Reading: The Learner's Needs and Self-Concepts," *The Florida Reading Quarterly*, June 1968, pp. 3-8.
2) *Clark, Kenneth and Clark, Maime, "Emotional Factors in Racial Identification and Reference in Negro Children," Journal of Negro Education*, 1950, pp. 341-50.

3) Morland, Kenneth. "Racial Acceptance and Preference of Nursery School Children in a Southern City," *Merrill-Palmer Quarterly of Behavior and Development*, Vol. VIII, 1962, p. 279.

4) Poussaint, Alvin. "Building a Strong Self-Image in Black Children," *Ebony Magazine*, August 1974, pp. 138-43.

5) Ward, Susan and Braun, John. "Racial Attitude among Black Youths," *Ebony Magazine*, Aug. 1974, p. 140.

6) DuBois, W.E.B., *The Soul of Black Folks*. N.Y.: New American Library, 1969, p. 45.

7) Black Child Care Conference, Columbus, Ohio, September 1981.

8) Gibran, Kahlil. *The Prophet*. N.Y.: Knopf, 1923, pp. 17-18.

9) Perkins, Eugene. *Home is a Dirty Street*. Chicago: Third World Press, 1974, pp. 26, 46.

10) Postman, Neil. *The Disappearance of Childhood*. N.Y.: Delacorte Press, N.Y. 1982, pp. 78-79.

11) Mander, Jerry. *Four Arguments for the Elimination of Television*. N.Y.: Quill, 1978, pp. 242-243.

12) Mathis, Sharon Bell. "True/False Messages for the Black Child," *Black Books Bulletin*, Vol. 2, Winter 1974, p. 19.

13) Jones, Richard. "Selecting Literature for Black Pre-School Children in Today's Society." *Black Child Journal*, Vol. 4, No. 1, 1982, pp. 13-14.

14) Gayle, Addison. *The Black Aesthetic*. N.Y.: Dell, 1970, pp. 352-353.

15) Campbell, Bebe Moore. "What Happened to the Afro?" *Ebony*, pp. 79-86.

16) Perkins, Stauton. *Satan in The Pulpit*. Rocky Mount: SES Development, 1981, p. 13.

17) Karenga, Maulana. *Kwanzaa: Origin, Concepts, Practice*. Los Angeles: Kawaida Publication, 1977, pp. 40-45.

CHAPTER 3

1) Goodlad, John. *A Place Called School*. N.Y.: McGraw Hill, 1984, p. 77.

2) Ibid, p. 12.

3) Friere, Paulo, *Pedagogy of the Oppressed*. N.Y.: Continuum, 1970, pp. 59-63.

4) Glasser, William. *Schools Without Failure*. N.Y.: Harper & Row, 1968, pp. 29, 30, 36.

5) Burns, Marilyn, "Making Sense out of Word Problems." *Learning*, 1981, pp. 26-32.

6) Ibid, p. 27.

7) Glasser, pp. 59-61.

8) Wilson, Amos. *The Developmental Psychology of the Black Child*. N.Y.: Africana Research Publ., 1978, p. 46.

9) Boykin, A.W. "Psychological/Behaviorial verve in Academic Task Performance," *The Journal of Negro Education* 1978, Vol. 42, #4, pp. 343-354.

10) Morgan, Harry. "How Schools Fail Black Children." *Social Policy*, Jan.–Feb. 1980, pp. 49–54.
11) Akbar, Na'im. "Cultural Expressions of the African American Child." *Black Child Journal*, Vol. 2 #2, 1981, p.10.
12) Hale, Janice. *Black Children, Their Roots, Culture, and Learning Styles.* Provo: Brigham Young University Press: 1982, p. 32–35.
13) Johnson, Robert. "Blacks in Science & Technology." Washington University, St. Louis, pp. 7–8.
14) Cultural Linguistic Approach Brochure. "Doing it Right the First Time," Chicago: Northeastern Illinois University Center for Inner City Studies, 1979.
15) The Future of Reading, *Families*, March, 1982, p. 56.
16) Flesch, Rudolf. *Why Johnny Can't Read*, N.Y.: Perennial p. 75.
17) Ibid, pp. 77–78.
18) U.S. Dept. of Education, "Is Your Child a Creative Thinker." *Good Parenting*, 1982, p.5.
19) Karenga, Maulana. *Kwanzaa, Origin, Concepts, Practice.* Los Angeles: Kawaida Publication, pp. 40–44.

CHAPTER 4

1) *St. Louis American*, June 21, 1979, p.3.
2) Gallup, G.H. "The Eleventh Annual Gallup." *Phi Delta Kappan*, 1979, (61) pp. 33–45.
3) Karenga, Maulana. *Introduction To Black Studies.* Los Angeles: Kawaida, Publication, 1982, pp. 206–212.
4) Postman, Neil. *The Disappearance of Childhood.* N.Y.: Delacorte, 1982, p. 134.
5) Vasiloff, Barbara. "Discipline: The Challenge of the 80s." *Today's Catholic Teacher*, October 1983, p.34.
6) An unpublished survey made by the author.
7) Skinner, B.F. *Beyond Freedom & Dignity.* N.Y.: Bantam, 1971, p. 16.
8) Kunjufu, Jawanza. *Children Are the Reward of Life.* Chicago: Afro-Am, 1980, pp. 6–7.
9) Canter, Lee. "Assertive Discipline." *Today's Catholic Teacher*, October 1983, pp. 36–37.
10) Chicago Public Schools. "Uniform Discipline Code." Chicago Board of Education, September, 1981, pp. 3–6.

CHAPTER 5

1) *Health Crusade*, Vol. #8, Oct. 1979, p. 9.
2) Colt, Allan, "Orthomolecular Approach to the Treatment of Children with Behavioral disorders and Learning Disabilities." *Journal of Applied Nutrition*, 1973, Vol. 25, Nos. 1&2, Winter, pp. 15–24.
3) Guyton, Arthur. *Textbook of Medical Physiology.* W.B. Saunders Company, 1971, pp. 872–885.
4) Gyorsy, Paul. "Bio-Chemical Aspects" in Symposium: The Uniqueness of Human Milk. *American Journal of Clinical Nutrition*, 1971, Vol. 24, No. 8, August, pp. 970–975.

5) Mander, Jerry. *Four Arguments for the Elimination of Television*. N.Y.: Quill, 1977, pp. 53, 115, 157, 263.
6) Ibid, pp. 171, 176, 206–208.
7) Ann Landers. *Chicago Sun Times*, May 1, 1984, p. 44.
8) *Washington Post*, May 1978, p. 4.

CHAPTER 6

1) National Black Child Development Institute. "Budget Cuts and Black Children," 1984.
2) Edmonds, Ronald. "Effective Schools for the Urban Poor." *Educational Leadership*, October, 1979, p. 16–22.
3) Ibid, pp. 17–18, 22.
4) Brookover, Wilbur. *Creating Effective Schools*. Holmes Beach: Learning Publications, 1982, pp. 32–33, 40.
5) Ibid, pp. 65–67
6) Goodlad, John. *A Place Called School*. N.Y.: McGraw-Hill, 1984, p. 18.
7) Ibid, p. 132.
8) Brookover, p. 149.
9) Goodlad, pp. 133–134.
10) Goodlad, pp. 152, 154, 155, 159, 297.
11) Dixon, Leon. "A Model For Aiding the Education of Black Children." Unpublished organizational manual.
12) Kunjufu, Jawanza. *Countering the Conspiracy to Destroy Black Boys*. Chicago: Afro-Am, 1982, p. 34.
13) Direct interview, United Negro College Fund Research Department, May 17, 1984.
14) Afrik, Hannibal. *Education for Self Reliance*. Stanford: Council of Independent Black Institutions, 1981, pp. 14, 16, 17.
15) Brookover, p. 203.
16) Voss, Gray. "Apple Diagnosed Intelligence Shatters IQ," *Softalk Magazine*, October 1981, p. 4.
17) Goodlad, p. 326.

Index

PLEDGE TO PARENTS

Thank you for bringing me into this world.
I look to you for love, guidance and wisdom.
You are my first and best role model.
I will do what you tell me to do.
I will always respect you.
All I ask, is that you understand,
I'm a child trying to grow in a world
Not fit for children.

JAWANZA KUNJUFU

PLEDGE FROM PARENTS

Thank you for coming into this world.
I will always love you and give you positive direc-
tion.
I understand I am your role model
And you're watching everything I do.
I will listen to you with respect.
All I ask, is that you understand
That before I was blessed with you
I had never been a parent.

JAWANZA KUNJUFU

SCHOOL SETS

Children's Library (best collection of Black children's books ever assembled), Grades K-8, 260 books, SECL . . . $2,999.95

Complete Set (SETCLAE), 190 books, 230 posters, 12 videos, 5 games and puzzles and much more! *(specify grade)*, SEC . . . $2,979.00

Black History Curriculum Basic Set (SETCLAE), 67 books, teachers' manual, and other products, *(specify grade)*, SEBH . . . $679.95 each

Anti-Bullying School Kit of 30 books plus teacher's manual . . . $399.95, *(specify grade 3-12)*

President Obama Set of 60 books and 3 posters: Obama Set . . . $749.95 *(free shipping)*

Educators' Library 28 books, SEEDL . . . $299.95

Hip Hop Street Curriculum: Dropout Prevention/Motivation 80 assorted books and teachers' manual, *(specify grade*, grades 5-H.S.), HHST . . . $799.95 each

Male In-house School Suspension 50 books, *(specify grade)*, SEM . . . $399.95 each

Female In-House School Suspension 50 books, *(specify grade)*, SEF . . . $399.95 each

Black History & Cultural Videos (10 Pack, VHS Only), MIV1 . . . $199.95

Hispanic History & Culture 50 books plus posters, HHCV . . . $419.95

Posters Set (230), SECP . . . $399.99 (non-returnable unless damaged)

Biographies set of 25 Famous African Americans Paperback, BI01 . . . $349.95

Biographies set of 16 Famous African Americans Paperback, BI02 . . . $159.95

Parent Set 28 books SECPA . . . $299.95

Math Set (Elementary), 30 books, 2 videos, and 2 games, SEMA-EL . . . $599.95

Math Set (High School), 30 books, 5 videos, 1 game ..., SEMA-HS . . . $599.95

Respect/Manners/Home Training 25 books (Hispanic K-8, Biographies 4-12, Character 4-12 and Classics 6-12), RMH-SET . . . $199.95

Best Books for Boys/Girls: Motivational Reading Books for At-risk Males & Females (20 Books), *(specify gender and grade)*: SEMR . . . $299.95

Character Developing Books for Youth Set (10 elementary books), CD400 . . . $129.95

H.S. Classics Set of 20 famous black books, CL500 . . . $279.95

High School Motivation Set of 18 books . . . $209.95

Pre-School Basic Set of 20 books . . . $159.95

Pre-School Complete Set of 60 books, 3 videos, 2 cd's and 2 dolls . . . $669.95

Black History Games (5) and **Black History Puzzles** (5) . . . $199.95

Complete School Set 556 children and adult books, 20 audios and 10 videos: SCHSET . . . $20,699.95

Free Shipping! (for a limited time only)
Prices are subject to change without notice.

Purchase now - before your grant monies expire.

How do your teachers feel about staff development?
Excited? Rejuvenated? Informed? Inspired?
How can you reduce teacher turnover?

Invite Dr. Kunjufu...

Best-selling author and consultant to most urban school districts.
Choose from these exciting workshops:

☐Closing the Racial Academic Achievement Gap
☐What are Best Practices for Black/Hispanic Males
☐Improving Minority Math Scores
☐Improving Minority Reading Test Scores
☐20 Traits of Master Teachers
☐Male Special Education Reduction
☐Single Gender Classrooms
☐Helping Teachers Bond with Black Students
☐Understanding Black Cultural Learning Styles
☐Developing a Relevant Curriculum
☐Principal Leadership Training
☐Reducing Negative Peer Pressure
☐Dr. King's Class on Conflict Resolution
☐Malcolm X Class on In-house Suspension
☐An African Centered Response to Ruby Payne's Poverty Theory
☐Parent Empowerment
☐Student Motivation Assemblies
☐Classroom Management
☐Classroom Observations

RESERVE YOUR DATE AND TIME SOON!

☐90 minutes ☐3 hours ☐5 hours

For additional information please contact
Ms. Smith, customersvc@africanamericanimages.com, (708) 672-4909

For each staff member order
"100 and 200 Plus Educational Strategies to Teach Children of Color"
for your staff and receive a *30%* discount * **$20.93** for *both* books.
Free Shipping

Purchase orders must exceed $150.00.

African American Images ♦ P.O. Box 1799 ♦ Chicago Heights, IL 60412 ♦ 1-800-552-1991 ♦ Fax 708-672-0466
www.AfricanAmericanImages.com ♦ e-mail address: customersvc@africanamericanimages.com

Dr. Jawanza Kunjufu invites you to

"Educating the Black and Hispanic Male National Conference"
Every first Tuesday and Wednesday in May

Conducted by *Dr. Jawanza Kunjufu*

▶ Only 12% of Black and Hispanic boys are proficient in reading

▶ How can we reduce the number of African American and Hispanic males in special education?

▶ How can we reduce their suspension and dropout rate?

▶ How can we increase their GPA?

▶ How can we motivate boys to value academics and to enjoy reading and improve reading scores?

▶ Understanding male learning styles

WHERE: Hilton Hotel, 9333 S. Cicero Ave., Oak Lawn, IL 60453 *(The hotel is 20 minutes from Chicago Midway airport.)*
*DAY 1: 9:30a.m. - 3:00p.m.
*DAY 2: 8:30a.m. - 2:00p.m.
*Call early to receive discounted hotel rates.

Tour of Urban Prep Male Charter School

The total cost is **$295.00** per person (*$249.95 for group of 10 or more if paid 2 months prior to conference*)!
Early bird special is **"$275.00"** *per person!* ❖ Bring your *"entire"* staff!

To Register you may complete the registration form and mail it with your payment to: African American Images, Inc, P.O. Box 1799, Chicago Heights, IL 60412. For additional information, or to register by phone, please contact Alicia at 708-672-4909 x731, aarcher@africanamericanimages.com. Add $10.00 *if paying at the door.* PAYMENTS ARE NON-REFUNDABLE, BUT MAY BE APPLIED TOWARD FUTURE CONFERENCE DATES. A CONTINENTAL BREAKFAST AND LUNCH WILL BE PROVIDED.
Please contact the Hilton Hotel at (708) 425-7800 for discounted room rates.

Name: _____ Name of School: _____
Address: _____
City: _____ State: _____ Zip code: _____
Daytime telephone #: _____ Evening telephone #: _____
E-mail *(required)*: _____

FORM OF PAYMENT: Official Purchase Order/Check/Credit Card

Credit Card _____ EXP Date _____ VERIFICATION #: _____
Signature & billing address required for credit card payments.

*****Can't make the conference? Invite Dr. Kunjufu to speak to your staff.*****
☐90 minutes ☐3 hours ☐4.5 hours *Email customersvc@africanamericanimages.com to book your date.
*****Buy the 5 book workshop set for $99.95 which includes the following:** *Understanding Black Male Learning Styles **
Reducing the Black Male Dropout Rate * Keeping Black Boys Out of Special Education *
Countering the Conspiracy to Destroy Black Boys (Series) * Raising Black Boys * plus Handouts and Quizzes
(Add $9.95 for shipping. Purchase Orders must exceed $150.00.)***

AFRICAN AMERICAN IMAGES, INC.
P.O. Box 1799 ♦ Chicago, Heights, IL 60412 ♦ (708) 672-4909 (phone) ♦ (708) 672-0466 (fax)
customersvc@africanamericanimages.com (e-mail) ♦ www.africanamericanimages.com (website)